DETERMINED

DETERMINED

THE 400-YEAR STRUGGLE FOR BLACK EQUALITY

Karen A. Sherry

Preface by the Rev. Grady W. Powell

Virginia Museum of History & Culture,
in association with D Giles Limited

Determined: The 400-Year Struggle for Black Equality is published in conjunction with the eponymous traveling exhibition, touring Virginia beginning in January 2021.

© 2021 Virginia Historical Society

First published jointly in 2021 by GILES
An imprint of D Giles Limited
66 High Street,
Lewes, BN7 1XG, UK
gilesltd.com

ISBN: 978-1-911282-99-0
All rights reserved

For the Virginia Museum of History & Culture:

Editor and Project Manager: Graham T. Dozier, Publications Managing Editor

Images in this book from the collection of the Virginia Historical Society, which owns and operates the Virginia Museum of History & Culture, are credited as VMHC.

For D Giles Limited:

Copy-edited and proof-read by Jodi Simpson

Designed by Ocky Murray

Produced by GILES, an imprint of D Giles Limited
Printed in Europe

CONTENTS

FOREWORD AND ACKNOWLEDGEMENTS

JAMIE O. BOSKET

Several significant events in recent years have prompted Americans to further reckon with our nation's long and enduring history of systemic racism. The Virginia Museum of History & Culture (VMHC) is well situated to contribute to this reflection and progress. Founded in 1831 as the Virginia Historical Society, the VMHC is one of the oldest and largest history institutions in the country, with an unparalleled collection of more than nine million artifacts and a mission to preserve and interpret the Commonwealth's full and often complex history. Virginia and Virginians have played a central role in the history of American slavery, segregation, and desegregation, and the ongoing fight for racial equity.

Determined: The 400-Year Struggle for Black Equality addresses the urgent need for a greater understanding of the roots of racial inequalities in the United States. It provides a broad and accessible survey of 400 years of Black history in Virginia, from 1619 through 2020. This is a difficult and often painful story, but one that we must confront in order to face the challenges of today and create a better world for tomorrow. We hope that the remarkable Black Virginians featured in this publication inspire you to continue to push our nation toward its ideal that "*all* men are created equal."

This book grew out of a major exhibition of the same title, organized by the VMHC in 2019 as part of the statewide commemoration of the 1619 arrival of captive Africans in Virginia. Beginning in 2021, a condensed panel version of the exhibition began traveling to cultural and educational venues across the Commonwealth. Taken together, along with numerous programs over the past few years, these components constitute an undertaking that would not have been possible without the support of many individuals and organizations. It gives me, on behalf of the VMHC, great pleasure to thank them here.

Our 2019 marquee exhibition, *Determined*, benefited immensely from the guidance of our statewide Advisory Committee. The members of this panel generously shared their expertise and constructive criticism to shape the project's concepts and contents. We are also grateful to Altria, American Evolution™ (Virginia's 2019 Commemoration), Conrad Mercer Hall, Mr. and Mrs. G. Gilmer Minor III, Bank of America, and The Community Foundation for a greater Richmond—sponsors of the exhibition and numerous programs and educational activities the VMHC hosted as part of the 2019 commemoration.

The VMHC is fortunate to have a visionary Board of Trustees committed to supporting the kind of inclusive and important history embodied in *Determined*. The museum's talented and dedicated staff (present and past) helped with myriad aspects of this publication and the museum's own evolution. I especially wish to recognize the tireless effort and scholarship of Dr. Karen Sherry, VMHC curator and the overall champion of *Determined* in all its forms. Dr. Sherry, an accomplished historian, has bettered our organization as a result of her tremendous work over the past several years.

I am proud to acknowledge my colleagues for their leadership, guidance, and unwavering support of this work, including Andrew Talkov, Sr. Director of Curatorial Affairs, Adam Scher, Vice President for Collections & Exhibitions, as well as curators Dr. William M. S. Rasmussen and L. Paige Newman. For sharing their deep knowledge of our collections and helping with access to resources, many members of our Collections & Exhibitions Division played an important role, including Rebecca Rose, Heather Beattie, Stacy Rusch, Andrew Foster, Dale Kostelny, Bryan Condra, Eileen Parris, Paulette Schwarting, John McClure, Matthew Guillen, Anne McCrery, and Lara Belfield. A gifted group of emerging professionals provided research and administrative support, as well as fresh insights, including research assistant Brianna Kirk; curatorial interns Casey Ellis Johnson, Paige Sellars, and Peighton Young; and volunteer Andrew Lang. The museum's educators—Maggie Creech, Hailey Fenner, Sam Florer, Chris Van Tassel, and Christina Vida—were also a fount of great ideas and information. Troy Wilkinson took beautiful photographs of VMHC collections and Veronica Blanco secured image rights.

Adding to the many voices that contributed to *Determined*, this book additionally benefited greatly from the expertise and support of Selicia Allen, Elvatrice Belsches, Dr. Elizabeth Chew, Dr. John Coski, Emmanuel Dabney, Dr. Brian Daugherity, Dr. Michael Dickinson, Dr. Adam Ewing, Katherine Gruber, Mae Breckenridge Haywood, Ronald Hurst, Adele Johnson, Martha Katz-Hyman, Gregg Kimball, Dr. Mary Caton Lingold, Jessie MacLeod, Taylor McNeilly, Dr. Jan Meck, Dr. Robert K. Nelson, Cameron Patterson, Mark Person, Katherine Ridgway, Dr. Jalane Schmidt, Patricia Silence, Shaun Hester Spencer, Susan Stein, Brent Tarter, Tim Talbott, Dr. Robert Trent Vinson, and David Voelkel. The staff at the Library of Virginia, Virginia Commonwealth University Library, and University of Virginia Library also assisted our research efforts.

The Reverend Grady W. Powell, former museum trustee and long-time supporter of the VMHC and our efforts to showcase underrepresented history, as well as a lifelong champion of Black civil rights and racial harmony, graciously contributed a moving preface to this book. Drs. Jeffrey Kerr-Ritchie and Larissa Smith served as expert readers of a manuscript draft and provided insightful feedback. Graham Dozier tirelessly did double-duty as copy editor and project manager. At D Giles Limited, we thank Dan Giles, Allison McCormick, Louise Parfitt, Louise Ramsay, and Harry Ault for the production of this volume. The graphic aesthetic is indebted to the original exhibition design created by HealyKohler Design.

I am—as is the entire VMHC family—especially grateful to the individuals featured in this book and their family members who entrusted their stories to us.

Lastly, I wish to thank the VMHC's diverse and growing community: the members, guests, students, teachers, and others across the Commonwealth and the country who engage with the museum. You expect from us history that is authentic, responsible, and relevant, and this drives our work. This publication is dedicated to you in the hope that *Determined* helps to foster a shared commitment to creating equity for all.

Jamie O. Bosket
President & CEO
Virginia Museum of History & Culture

ADVISORY COMMITTEE

Dr. Edward L. Ayers
Tucker-Boatwright Professor
of the Humanities and
President Emeritus,
University of Richmond

Victor K. Branch
Senior Vice President,
Richmond Market President,
Bank of America

Rev. Benjamin P. Campbell
Pastor Emeritus, Richmond Hill
and Pastoral Associate, St. Paul's
Episcopal Church (Richmond)

Dr. Elizabeth Clark-Lewis
Professor of History,
Howard University

Dr. Spencer R. Crew
Clarence J. Robinson
Professor of History,
George Mason University

Dr. Claudrena N. Harold
Professor and Department Chair,
Corcoran Department of History,
University of Virginia

Dr. Julian Maxwell Hayter
Associate Professor of Leadership
Studies, University of Richmond

Dr. James Horn
President and CO, Jamestown
Rediscovery Foundation
Photo: Michael Lavin

Delegate Delores L. McQuinn
Virginia House of Delegates

Dr. Cassandra L. Newby-Alexander
Dean, College of Liberal Arts,
Norfolk State University

Justin G. Reid
Director, Community Initiatives,
Virginia Humanities
Photo: Peter Hedlund

Dr. Susan P. Schoelwer
Executive Director of Historic
Preservation and Collections and
Robert H. Smith Senior Curator,
George Washington's Mount Vernon

PREFACE

THE REV. GRADY W. POWELL

During my early teenage years in the 1940s, a public school teacher spoke to a gathering of rural church school representatives. Her subject was "The Need Is Great: The Time Is Now." The general message was twofold: first, emphasizing the importance of an education, particularly staying in school and studying diligently; second, encouraging an awareness of civil rights and social justice. These reflections came to mind as I read this amazing historical work. It speaks loudly of the teacher's topic—the need is great and the time is now to look at the past, ponder the present, and work for the future.

Most Americans will be shattered, as I was, when they read herein the many unknown events of human indignities in the 400-year history of Black people in Virginia. Readers will see in this account the philosophical question "If a tree falls in the forest and no one is around to hear it, does it make a sound?" The answer is a resounding yes. It takes time, however, for historians and scholars to forage through the dense forest of told and untold history and openly offer their findings.

Throughout this narrative, we encounter provocative stories of the worst of times and also periods of more elevated touches of humanity. Further, we view the struggle of individuals who, so to speak, were forced to make bricks without straw, and others who received unfathomably harsh and cruel punishments. For example, there is the 1708 incident of Bambara Harry and Dinah, who unsuccessfully attempted to escape enslavement by running away. Their enslaver, Robert "King" Carter, one of the wealthiest men in colonial Virginia, got permission from the court to punish them by cutting off their toes. Such atrocities and disregard for human lives—whether of African descent or otherwise—are far too numerous in our history.

In spite of the worst of times, my spirit is uplifted to read other accounts of individuals who pursued freedom and equality in unique ways despite the usual dangers. There was the enslaved man Henry "Box" Brown, who self-emancipated. He freed himself by building a crate and having his allies place him in it and then ship him to abolitionists in Philadelphia. Others sought empowerment for Black people, like Mary S. Peake, a free woman of color, who broke the law by teaching enslaved and free Black Virginians, and Anne Spencer, whose poetry expressed the type of world that so many like her faced during those years.

Among Virginia's more recent civil rights leaders included in this account are Maggie Lena Walker, John Mitchell, Jr., Barbara Johns Powell, Wyatt Tee Walker, L. Douglas Wilder, and others. Because of the fortitude and leadership of these and other individuals, they are unknown no longer in the record of our United States history. They indeed illustrate progress in the pursuit of equality.

For me, this book brings to light the persons and events of our shared past that were left in darkness within the Virginia history books that were available in my school. Those responsible for the content of information that I received deemed those missing pages of Black history not worthy of chronicling. What a blatant omission!

This marvelous book takes us back to 1619 when "20. and odd Negroes" were brought as slaves by English privateers to Point Comfort (now Hampton). The moving history of these and other enslaved Africans and their descendants—spanning more than 400 years—makes these pages such valued reading.

Yes, falling trees do make a sound. History, though unacknowledged, did happen. In this book, the Virginia Museum of History & Culture illuminates the past, sees the images, and hears the stories and sounds.

As one who has lived for more than three-quarters of a century, I can assure readers that this expansive work will help to fill those missing pages in the schoolbooks of my youth. Accordingly, this helps me put in perspective recent events, such as the murder of George Floyd, the removal of Confederate statues, and other occurrences. If the evil action recorded in history could be obliterated and replaced by ethical choices of the highest good, there would be no need for senseless killings. There never would have been a need for the statues that were erected in honor of people who fought a war to defend slavery. I see this book as a luminous and prophetic lighthouse for present and future generations. The content illuminates the stormy and treacherous seas of America's original sin with historical honesty. If we meet the present challenges, maybe, hopefully, all of humanity will rejoice, knowing that we shall overcome. This responsibility is for each generation. The teacher who spoke to us in the 1940s was right—the need is great: the time is now.

DETERMINED: THE 400-YEAR STRUGGLE FOR BLACK EQUALITY

INTRODUCTION

In the spring of 2020, the global coronavirus pandemic and the widespread social unrest in the wake of George Floyd's death by police laid bare the racial inequities in the United States. COVID-19 and the related economic fallout has disproportionately affected people of color, particularly since they are more likely to have frontline jobs that put them at greater risk of exposure and to suffer disparities in financial security and healthcare access compared to white Americans. The horrifying spectacle of a Minneapolis police officer kneeling on George Floyd's neck for more than nine minutes, indifferent to Floyd's desperate cries for breath, sent shockwaves around the world that ignited protests against police brutality and racial injustice.

The compounded impact of these two crises has pushed America to an inflection point—to a moment of national reckoning about race. The systemic racism that plagues our society has roots reaching back more than 400 years to 1619, when the first enslaved Africans were forcibly brought to the fledgling colony of Virginia, barely a decade after its founding. Their arrival marked a pivotal beginning of slavery in British North America and a legacy of race-based oppression and discrimination that reverberates to the present.

This book aims to contribute to this national reckoning by fostering a greater understanding of the history of race and racism in America— and, by extension, of how we got to this point. To this end, *Determined* presents a broad survey of four centuries of Black history in Virginia— history encompassing slavery and emancipation, segregation and the civil rights movement, the election of the first Black president, and the rise of Black Lives Matter. Throughout this complex history, an overarching theme has been that of struggle. Acting individually and collectively, Black people have fought *for* freedom, justice, and opportunity and *against* oppression, discrimination, and dehumanization.

Their efforts have brought meaningful changes to American society by forcing the nation to continuously reconsider the meaning of its highest ideals of democracy and universal equality.

The title, *Determined*, draws on a passage from Dr. Martin Luther King's final speech on April 3, 1968, the night before his assassination, in which he described the aims of the civil rights movement:

> We are determined to gain our rightful place in God's world. And that's all this whole thing is about. We aren't engaged in any negative protest and in any negative arguments with anybody. We are saying that we are determined to be men. We are determined to be people.[1]

The spirit of determination that King so emphatically declares has animated the centuries-long struggle for Black equity. "Determined" embodies the agency, persistence, and resilience of Black people and their allies engaged in this fight. This word also evokes ideas of influence, both the defining influence of skin color on an individual's social status and the profound impact Black people have had on the United States.

This book explores 400 years of the Black experience in Virginia through the stories of key individuals and events in the fight for Black equality. It is arranged chronologically into four chapters. The first chapter covers the colonial era, from the arrival of the first captive Africans to the eve of the American Revolution. During this period, the Virginia colony codified a system of race-based human bondage—against the backdrop of Black resistance—that spread throughout British North America. Chapter two traces Black Virginians' struggle for liberty from the Revolution through the Civil War. After the United States gained its independence, slavery was gradually abolished in the North while it grew more deeply entrenched in the South—a sectional divide that culminated in a bloody conflict that ended 246 years of slavery. From Reconstruction through World War II, the timeframe of chapter three, Black Americans experienced both progress and backlash. As they embraced the promises of freedom and new opportunities, they faced new forms of oppression, including segregation, disenfranchisement, and violent intimidation. Chapter four explores the modern era, from the civil rights movement of the 1950s and '60s through 2020. During this period, Black Americans gained legal equality and broke barriers in many arenas of American life, yet our society remains rife with systemic racism and persistent racial disparities.

Each chapter begins with an introductory essay followed by individual entries on Black Virginians who represent key aspects of the struggle for Black equality during that era, as well as related historical context. *Determined* features thirty-five men and women—a selection that is by necessity limited given the 400-year sweep of this book. Nevertheless, these highlighted figures reflect the diversity of the African American experience in Virginia, as well as diverse approaches to effecting change. By focusing on individual stories, this study underscores Black agency, the choices and actions people made to shape their world. To be sure, throughout American history, Black people have been subjected to myriad forms of oppression, yet they were *not* passive victims: they resisted in large and small ways and with varying degrees of success.

Despite certain limitations in its scope, *Determined* is not just a Virginia story or a Black story, but an American one. From the 1619 origins of American slavery to recent protests for racial justice, Virginia has always played a pivotal role in national race relations. Furthermore, Black history is inextricably entwined with American history as Black people have fundamentally influenced the country's economic, political, and cultural identity. In telling this American story, *Determined* commemorates the accomplishments and setbacks, the triumphs and sacrifices of the 400-year-long struggle for Black equality. It also sheds light on how we got to the events of 2020, and illuminates a path forward to achieve real equity for all Americans. As the writer James Baldwin said, "Nothing can be changed unless it is faced."[2] Ultimately, we hope that the stories you encounter here leave you determined to make a difference and to push our nation ever closer to becoming a more perfect union.

1

FIRST GENERATIONS, 1619–1775

CHAPTER 1:
FIRST GENERATIONS,
1619–1775

Beginnings

In January 1620, Jamestown settler and planter John Rolfe wrote to the Virginia Company of London reporting on conditions in the colony. His letter mentions an event from the preceding year that would profoundly shape the course of United States history:

> About the latter end of August, [the *White Lion*] arrived at Point-Comfort, the Comandors name Capt Jope. . . . He brought not any thing but 20. and odd Negroes, which the Governor and Cape Marchant bought for victuals (whereof he was in greate need as he pretended) at the best and easyest rates they could. . . . Three or 4. daies after the *Treasurer* arrived.[3]

Although sparse in details, Rolfe's letter documents the first recorded Africans in the Virginia colony. The *White Lion* and the *Treasurer* were British privateers that sailed around the Atlantic looking to loot Spanish and Portuguese ships carrying gold, silver, and other cargo. They arrived at Point Comfort (present-day Hampton), at the confluence of the Chesapeake Bay and the James River, after attacking a Portuguese slave ship bound for Mexico and making off with about 50 enslaved Africans divided between them. When they arrived in Virginia, the ship captains traded the "Negroes" for food with colonial officials (see entry on Angela, p. 26).

The historic nature of this event requires some qualification. These captives were *not* the first enslaved Africans in the Americas. Since around 1500, the Spanish and Portuguese had been transporting Africans to work—alongside enslaved Indigenous peoples—in their South and Central American colonies, including the Caribbean. Nor were the "20. and odd Negroes" the first in what would become the United

States or in the British colonies. The Spanish brought enslaved Africans on an expedition to present-day South Carolina in 1526, and the British colony of Bermuda was exploiting African labor by 1616.

Nevertheless, 1619 still marks an important turning point: the beginnings of Virginia's involvement in African slavery. As Britain's first permanent settlement in North America and as the largest and one of the most powerful of the original Thirteen Colonies, Virginia had a formative impact on the development of the United States. Over the next century and a half—the period covered by this chapter—Virginia codified a system of slavery that spread throughout these colonies and fundamentally influenced the economic, political, and cultural character of America.

Virginia's Evolution

In 1619, the Virginia colony was struggling to survive. A little more than a decade had passed since the 1607 founding of the Jamestown settlement, about 40 miles upriver from Point Comfort. Extreme hardships marked these early years, including starvation, disease, and poor management, as well as hostile relations with Native tribes of the Powhatan chiefdom. In the mid-1610s, settlers began cultivating tobacco—a crop that found great success throughout the Chesapeake region and high demand among European consumers.

Over the following decades, tobacco transformed Virginia from a fledgling outpost to a large, prosperous, and powerful colony. The plant became the basis of Virginia's economy, its primary export, and the source of wealth for plantation owners and those involved in the tobacco trade. Tobacco cultivation required a great deal of land and labor. White settlers expropriated Indian territory—often violently—and, by the late

17th century, Virginia's Indigenous peoples had been decimated and displaced onto reservations. The English colony expanded first along the James and then other rivers that emptied into the Chesapeake Bay, and later further west.

A labor-intensive crop, tobacco created a high demand for workers to clear land for planting, cultivate the plants, and harvest and process the leaves for shipping. Until around 1680, white indentured servants from Britain and Europe performed most of this work, along with a small percentage of enslaved Africans and Native Americans. These white

Joshua Fry and Peter Jefferson, *Map of the Most Inhabited Part of Virginia* (London: Thomas Jeffreys, 1751).

VMHC, Gift of Paul Mellon in 1999

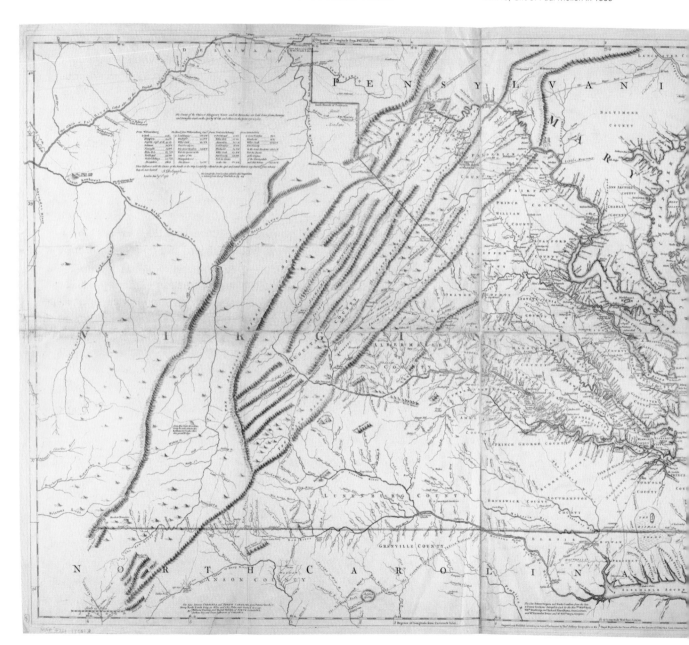

laborers contracted to work for an employer for a set number of years in exchange for their transatlantic voyage and food, shelter, and clothing. Despite harsh conditions, the promise of better opportunities drew many men and women to Virginia through indenture arrangements.

Beginning in 1618, the colonial government provided incentives to immigration by granting settlers fifty acres of land for each person or "head" transported to Virginia. This headright system benefited the wealthy, who amassed property by bringing indentured servants to the colony. It also created a society in which economic and political power was concentrated in the hands of elite planter families.

Virginia's labor force changed dramatically in the late 17th century. In 1680, the ratio of white indentured servants to enslaved Black people was four to one; by 1700, it was one to four.[4] Several factors contributed to this transformation, including Britain's deepening involvement in the transatlantic slave trade that increased both the supply and the profitability of slave labor. In addition, improved economic circumstances in England reduced the number of indentured servants willing to come to the colony. With the growing dependence on enslaved Black workers, Virginia evolved from a society with slaves to a slave society—that is, a society in which slavery was the dominant form of labor and the basis of social relationships.[5]

As part of this evolution, Virginia's white leadership, its colonial officials and powerful planters, systemized chattel slavery in law (*de jure*) and practice (*de facto*). The legislature and courts established a body of laws or "slave codes" that defined the status of "negroes," limited their rights and opportunities for freedom, and treated Black bondage as a lifelong condition (see entry on John Punch, and "Race and the Law," pp. 34, 37). Socio-legal divisions between the races became more rigid, and forced servitude came to be associated almost exclusively with Black skin. There were some free Black Virginians, but they made up a tiny percentage of the colony's population and they were also subjected to discrimination. For example, in 1723, the General Assembly passed a law stripping free Black men of the right to vote.[6]

VIRGINIA'S BLACK POPULATION (APPROXIMATE FIGURES), 1620–1770

Year	Number of Black people	Percentage of colony's population
1620	32	3 ½
1670	2,000	5 ½
1720	26,560	30
1770	187,600	42

Africans in Virginia

For several decades following 1619, the number of people of African descent in the colony was relatively small. But their numbers rose steeply from the late 1600s through the eve of the American Revolution, by which point they constituted more than 40 percent of Virginia's population (see fig.).[7] In 1660, Britain officially entered the African slave trade by creating a royally chartered company with a monopoly for supplying African slaves to its colonies in North America and the Caribbean. Other British merchants, including American colonists, were permitted to join the trade in 1698. Between 1700 and 1750, slave traders imported approximately 45,000 Africans to Virginia.[8] Natural increase through reproduction—enslaved women bearing children—also contributed to population growth.

As their numbers grew, people of African descent became deeply entwined in all aspects of Chesapeake life. Their labors—as well as their technological knowledge brought from Africa in agriculture, metal work, and other trades—fueled Virginia's development. They also influenced social and legal systems, as well as its culture. Africans had an especially profound impact in Virginia, which throughout America's history of slavery had the largest enslaved population of any colony or state.

What of the lives of people of African descent in colonial Virginia? Historical records are sparse, making it difficult to know even the most basic biographical information, such as names, life dates, and places of origin. Colonial archives, kept by white officials and enslavers, generally do not record Black stories or do so in only fragmentary form. There are no extant first-hand accounts until the late 18th century (see entry on Olaudah Equiano, p. 29).

Despite such archival silences, it is possible to sketch the general contours of the experiences of Black people in colonial Virginia. Most

Gourd fiddle, 19th century—derived from the West African *mbanza*, this type of instrument is a predecessor of the American banjo.
Courtesy of the Blue Ridge Institute & Museum of Ferrum College

of them labored on plantations, cultivating fields, tending livestock, and maintaining the planter's household. They also worked in the homes and shops and along the wharves of the colony's developing towns and ports. Initially, there was a certain amount of social fluidity among bound laborers, with enslaved Africans and white indentured servants often working and living side-by-side. But as slavery became more codified, racial separation became more rigid.

On large plantations with large workforces, enslaved people formed familial and social ties—ties that provided some respite from the brutalities of slavery. Even though these enslaved communities were composed of Africans from diverse ethnic backgrounds, they fostered the sharing and preservation of native cultural traditions, including foodways and spiritual and musical practices. In turn, these African traditions influenced the development of a unique American culture. For example, African words such as *okra* and *goober* (peanut) became part of the American vocabulary, and the West African *mbanza* became the American banjo.

The individuals featured in this chapter represent the varied experiences of people of African descent in colonial Virginia from 1619 to 1775. Their lives, often marked by oppression and injustice, reflect Virginia's evolution into a slave society. At the same time, these stories showcase Black resistance and underscore the fundamental human desire for freedom and equality.

FIRST ARRIVAL

ANGELA (LIFE DATES UNKNOWN)

Angela, also spelled Angelo, was among the first recorded Africans forcibly brought to Virginia in 1619—and one of the few First Arrivals for which we have a name. Little else is known about her life, except that she endured the violence, dislocation, and trauma of the international slave trade, as well as bondage in the early English settlement. Angela was likely from the Ndongo kingdom of West Central Africa (present-day Angola), where people spoke Kimbundu and raised crops and cattle. Portugal had been trading with the Ndongo and Kongo peoples of this region since the 1480s, but relations turned increasingly violent in the late 16th century as the Portuguese waged war to gain control of the supply of enslaved labor for European colonies in the Americas. In the 17th century, this region became the primary source of slaves shipped to the New World.[9]

Angela was kidnapped in the violent raids launched by the Portuguese and their African allies in 1618–1619. With thousands of other captives, she was forced to march more than 150 miles to the coastal city of Luanda and its slave jails. She was likely baptized as required by the Portuguese—which might account for her Christian name—before being loaded onto the *São João Bautista*. Heavily laden with a cargo of 350 captives, the slave ship set sail for Veracruz, New Spain (Mexico). In the Gulf of Mexico, two British privateers—the *White Lion* and *Treasurer*—attacked the *São João Bautista*, stole about fifty Africans, and sailed for the English colony of Virginia.

In late August 1619, the *White Lion* landed at Point Comfort (present-day Hampton) with its cargo of "20. and odd Negroes." The ship's captain sold these Africans for food supplies to the colony's governor and cape merchant (head merchant). A few days later, the *Treasurer* arrived with additional captives. Angela was on this second ship and was likely purchased by Captain William Pierce, a wealthy merchant

Map of West Central
Africa in 1619

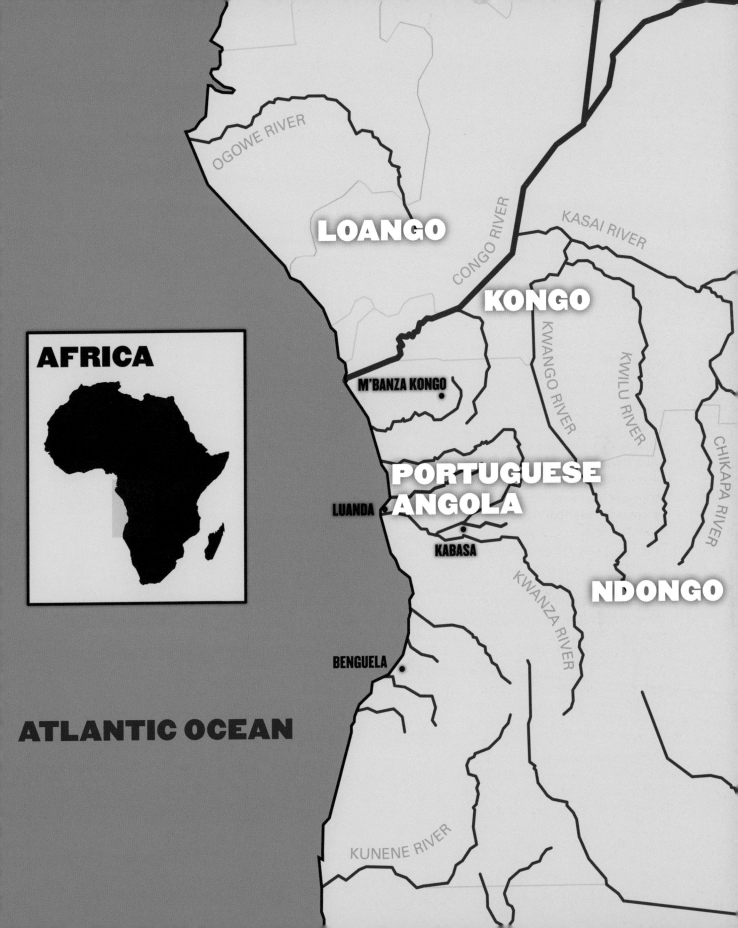

and official. The 1625 census of the Virginia colony lists "Angelo [Angela] a Negro Woman in the *Treasuror*" living in Pierce's household in Jamestown, along with his wife, Joan, and three white indentured servants (see fig.).[10]

The First Arrivals had to endure forced labor and the harsh conditions of the young settlement, including "seasoning" (adapting to new environments and new diseases) and the Powhatan Indian attack of 1622. The twenty-three Africans recorded in the 1625 census were scattered among the households of wealthy planters and colonial leaders that stretched along the James River. In the Pierce household, Angela likely helped with the cooking, cleaning, and tending of gardens. As the only African living there, she was undoubtedly lonely and mourning her lost family and homeland. We do not know when she died, but we can assume she must have been tenacious to survive so many hardships. The 1619 arrival of Angela and other Angolans marked both the beginning of slavery in Virginia and the beginning of African influence on American culture—legacies that still resonate today.

William Pierce's household (detail), from *Muster of the Inhabitants* of Virginia (1625).

The National Archives of the UK, ref. CO1/3(136v)

An Angolan woman, illustration from Giovanni Antonio Cavazzi, *Istorica descrizione de' tre' regni Congo, Matamba et Angola* (Bologna: Giacomo Monti, 1687).

The Newberry Library, Chicago

THE INTERNATIONAL NETWORKS OF SLAVERY

OLAUDAH EQUIANO (1745–1797)

Olaudah Equiano's 1789 autobiography provided one of the earliest and most famous accounts of slavery in the Atlantic world by an African writer. He relates how, at age eleven, slavers kidnapped him from his Ibo village (in present-day Nigeria) and sold him into bondage. From Africa, Equiano was sent briefly to Barbados and then to Virginia, where he worked on a tobacco plantation. He spent the next decade sailing around the world with subsequent owners, a British naval officer and a Philadelphia merchant involved in the slave trade. Equiano also learned to read and write and converted to Christianity.

In 1766, at age twenty-one, he purchased his freedom with money he earned selling goods in various ports. As a free Briton, he continued his far-flung travels—including an Arctic expedition—before settling in London. Here, Equiano became active in the burgeoning abolition movement as part of the Sons of Africa, a group of free Black men who campaigned to end slavery. He wrote *The Interesting Narrative of the Life of Olaudah Equiano, or Gustavus Vassa, the African*, and reaped the rewards of its great success—it went through nine editions in English before his 1797 death and was translated into several foreign languages.

Equiano led an extraordinary life of slavery and freedom, of seafaring adventures and international fame. Yet his autobiography captures the common experience of millions of Africans who were kidnapped from their homelands, sold into slavery, and transported to the Americas. Some historians question Equiano's African origin, but his vivid accounts of the slave trade have the ring of truth from either firsthand knowledge or a faithful recounting.[11] One particularly striking episode from the *Narrative* is his description of the miserable conditions in the cargo hold during the Middle Passage, the transatlantic voyage from African to American ports:

The stench of the hold . . . became absolutely pestilential. The closeness of the place and the heat of the climate, added to the number in the ship, which was so crowded that each had scarcely room to turn himself, almost suffocated us . . . the air soon became unfit for respiration from a variety of loathsome smells, and brought on a sickness amongst the slaves, of which many died.

In another section, the author recalls the disorientation of his early days of enslavement on the Virginia plantation of a "Mr. Campbell." The young Equiano felt the loneliness of the language barrier, of having "no person to speak to that I could understand," as well as fear at his strange new surroundings. Upon his first encounter with a portrait painting, he assumed that it contained the spirit of Campbell's dead ancestor because the image "appeared constantly to look at me."[12]

Equiano's autobiography had a profound impact on the abolition movement in Britain and America—introducing many white audiences to both the horrors of slavery and the humanity of its victims. As a pioneering example of the slave narrative, his *Narrative* also influenced other Black writers of this genre, including Frederick Douglass, whose own 1845 autobiography similarly galvanized antislavery sentiment.

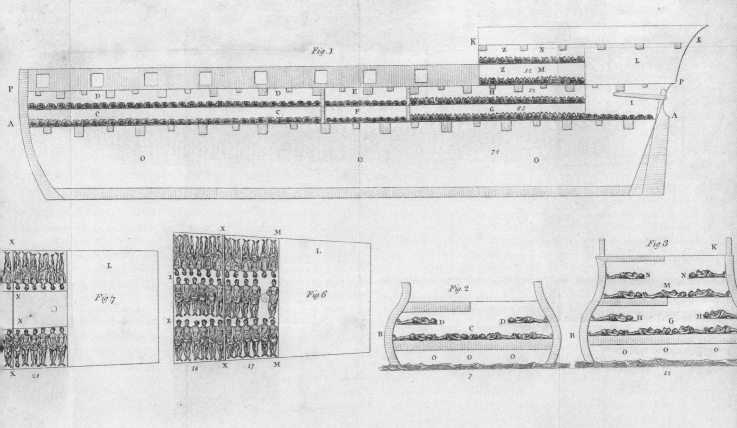

Fig. 1

Fig. 7

Fig. 6

Fig. 2

Fig. 3

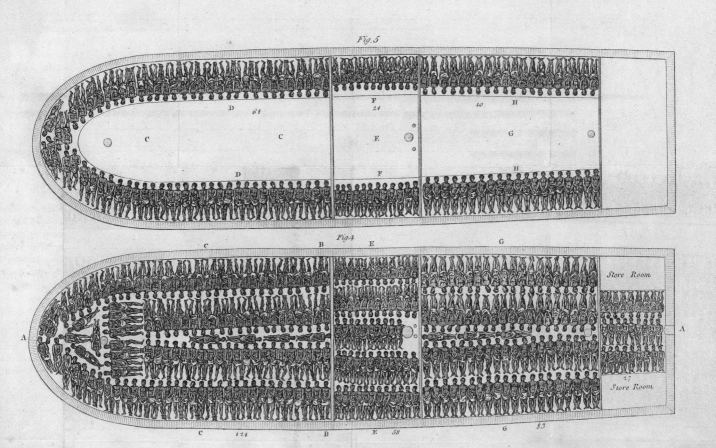

Fig. 5

Fig. 4

Store Room

Store Room

Hamsley sculp.

THE TRIANGLE TRADE

NEW WORLD AGRICULTURAL PRODUCTS (HARVESTED BY ENSLAVED LABOR) TO EUROPEAN MARKETS

EUROPEAN GOODS TO WEST AFRICA TO EXCHANGE FOR SLAVES

ENSLAVED PEOPLE TO THE AMERICAS

36,000

Transatlantic voyages
made by slave ships

1 – 3

Number of months
a voyage took

The "Middle Passage"
from Africa to the Americas
constitutes the second or
middle leg of the triangular trade
route of European ships.

250 – 600

Captive Africans
on each ship

1 in 10

Voyages had a
slave revolt

The slave trade linked Europe, Africa, and the Americas in a highly profitable yet morally repugnant network of human trafficking. Between 1525 and 1865, European and American slavers and their African allies kidnapped, sold, and transported millions of diverse African peoples across the Atlantic Ocean. This diaspora—the removal of people from their homelands—constitutes one of the largest forced migrations in human history.[13]

Untold numbers of victims died in the forced marches to the coast, in the barracoons or jails awaiting boarding, and in the densely packed and disease-ridden cargo holds of slave ships. The people who survived the transatlantic crossing worked in the fields, mines, ports, shops, and homes of European settlements in the New World. Their labors built colonies throughout the Americas and the fortunes of Western powers and individuals involved in this system. Enslaved Africans also transformed American cultures through the influence of their language, foodways, spiritual practices, and musical traditions.

AFRICAN SLAVERY BY THE NUMBERS
Total of 12.5 million Africans boarded onto slave ships

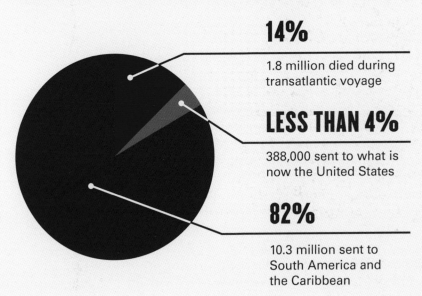

14%
1.8 million died during transatlantic voyage

LESS THAN 4%
388,000 sent to what is now the United States

82%
10.3 million sent to South America and the Caribbean

CODIFYING SLAVERY

JOHN PUNCH (LIFE DATES UNKNOWN)

For several decades following their 1619 arrival, people of African descent made up a small portion of Virginia's population—only about 2 percent in 1650. Indentured servants from Britain and other European countries provided the majority of the colony's labor. These servants entered into a contract or indenture in which they agreed to work for four to seven years for an employer in exchange for their transatlantic passage and food, clothing, and housing. Bound laborers—indentured whites and enslaved Blacks—toiled side-by-side in the tobacco fields, socialized and slept together, and faced the same harsh conditions. They also sometimes rebelled together.

Despite these shared interracial experiences of servitude, people of African descent were treated differently from whites in early colonial Chesapeake—they were *not* indentured servants as some history books have suggested. Enslaved Black people did not choose their lot: they rarely had indenture contracts or gained their freedom. In practice, Virginia society treated servants of African descent as slaves—held in bondage for life and considered property—even before slavery was fully defined in British law. The racial differentiation among servants is evident in the colony's first census of 1620, which included white indentured servants among the 885 English inhabitants and, in a separate count, the thirty-two "Negroes" and four "Indians" who were "in the service of the English."[14]

John Punch, a Black man, was part of a court decision that began the legal codification of slavery. In 1640, he and two white indentured servants ran away from Hugh Gwyn, a wealthy planter in Charles City County. Their motivations are unknown: they might have been seeking freedom for its own sake or trying to escape back-breaking labor, meager provisions, and abusive treatment. They were caught in Maryland and returned to Virginia to face punishment. The General

John Singleton Copley, *Head of a Negro*, 1777 or 1778, oil on canvas.
Detroit Institute of Arts, Founders Society Purchase, Gibbs-Williams Fund, 52.118

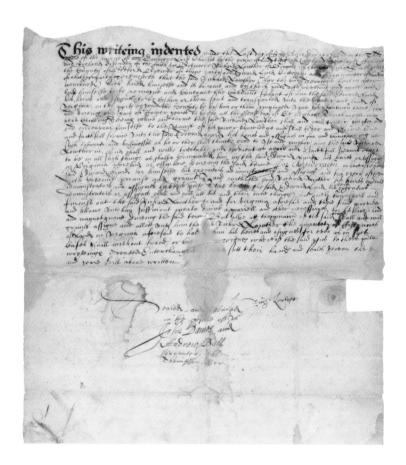

Court sentenced all three men to a whipping of "thirty stripes apiece." In addition:

> One called Victor, a Dutchman, the other a Scotchman called James Gregory, shall first serve out their times with their master according to their Indentures, and one whole year apiece after the time of their service is Expired. By their said Indentures in recompense of [Gwyn's] Loss sustained by their absence and after that service to their said master is Expired to serve the colony for three whole years apiece, and that the third being a negro named John Punch shall serve his said master or his assigns for the time of his natural Life here or elsewhere.[15]

While the white servants received four additional years of indenture (one to their master and three to the colony), the court sentenced the "negro" to lifetime service to Hugh Gwyn. This is John Punch's only appearance in the historical record—nothing else is known of his life.

His case marks the first time Virginia law distinguished between people of European and African descent in sentencing and defined lifetime bondage for "negroes." Over the following decades, Virginia fully codified the institution of slavery in both customs and laws.

[above left] Indenture agreement between Richard Lowther of Bedfordshire, England, and Edward Lyurd of Virginia, July 31, 1627.
VMHC, Gift of Preston Davie

[above right] Whipping post from a jail yard in Portsmouth, Virginia, 19th century.
VMHC, Gift of the Yates County Historical Society

Slaves in Court 1741,
19th century, illustration.
Granger

When Africans were first brought to Virginia, African slavery was new in British territories and, therefore, not covered by existing law. Colonial courts and legislators created a body of regulations defining the status of "negroes" and policing their behavior. In general, these laws were:

- **Reactive**—they developed in response to acts of Black rebellion or assertions of rights
- **Restrictive**—they stripped rights away from Black people rather than granted privileges
- **Discriminatory**—they codified racial difference and privileged white people.

Some enslaved Virginians sought their freedom through the courts, but colonial authorities quickly closed off legal avenues to freedom. Black people continued to resist bondage by running away and plotting rebellion, prompting lawmakers to legislate repeatedly on these actions.

Over the course of the colonial period, Virginia's "slave codes" evolved into a systematic body of regulations and became a model throughout America's original Thirteen Colonies.[16]

SOME EARLY LAWS ENACTED BY THE VIRGINIA GOVERNMENT

1640 John Punch sentenced to lifetime servitude

1662 A child follows the enslaved or free status of the mother

1667 Baptism cannot be used to free an enslaved person

1669 A master who kills his slave will be exempt from prosecution

1670 Free Black and Indigenous people prohibited from owning white servants

1680 Enslaved individuals prohibited from carrying weapons, assembling in large groups, and traveling off plantations without permission; similar measures to prevent slave revolt passed in 1682 and 1691

1691 Interracial marriage outlawed

1705 "An Act concerning Servants and Slaves" consolidates many earlier laws into a comprehensive slave code and declares "all Negro, mulatto, and Indian slaves . . . shall be held to be real estate"

SUING FOR FREEDOM

ELIZABETH KEY (1630–BEFORE 1667)

Elizabeth Key (later Grinsted Parse) represents one of the rare instances in which a person with African ancestry was able to gain her freedom in early colonial Virginia—and she did so by exploiting certain legal ambiguities around race at the time. Elizabeth was the daughter of Thomas Key (or Kaye), an English planter and burgess for Denby (present-day Newport News), and an unnamed enslaved woman he "owned."

In 1636, as Key and his English wife were preparing to return to England, he bound Elizabeth into service for nine years to Humphrey Higginson, who was to provide her with food and clothing, then free her when she reached age fifteen. At some point, Higginson transferred Elizabeth's indenture to John Mottrom, a planter in Northumberland County. At the time of Mottrom's death in 1655, she was still in service—more than ten years after the term specified by her now-late father.

In January 1656, Elizabeth Key—identified as a "mulatto"—sued Mottrom's estate in the county court for freedom for herself and her infant son, John. She based her lawsuit on several claims: that her father was a free Englishman, that she was a Christian, and that her service was bound by an indenture agreement that had expired. It is unknown why she waited so long to challenge her bondage; perhaps having her own child prompted her to secure freedom for both of them. The court ruled in her favor, but Mottrom's estate successfully challenged this decision.

Elizabeth appealed to the House of Burgesses, which then acted as the colony's highest court of appeals. The Burgesses decided that "by the Common Law the Child of a Woman slave begot by a freeman ought to bee free" and that, as compensation for her extra years of service, "her last Master [Mottrom] should give her Corne and Cloathes."[17]

"A Slave Father Sold Away from His Family" (detail), illustration from *The Child's Anti-Slavery-Book* (New York: Carlton & Porter, 1860).
Photo by Library of Congress/Corbis/VCG via Getty Images

Jack Clifton, *The First
Legislative Assembly in
Virginia Met at Jamestown in
1619*, 1968, acrylic on canvas.
Courtesy of the Library of Virginia

Ultimately, Elizabeth's father's status as a free Englishman determined
her own free status.

Upon gaining her freedom, Elizabeth married William Grinsted,
a white farmer who had also worked in Mottrom's household. He
represented her in court and was the father of John and her subsequent
children. After his death, she married John Parse. His 1667 will implies
that she died before him.[18]

Although Elizabeth Key won her freedom suit, her success had
unfortunate implications. Virginia's legal system adapted to make it
increasingly difficult for people with African ancestry to gain freedom. No
doubt in response to her case, the House of Burgesses passed a statute
in 1662 that reversed centuries of British common law by declaring a
child's status followed that of the mother. This law tacitly acknowledged
the sexual exploitation of enslaved women by white men, as well as the
threat posed to slavery if mixed-race children could gain freedom based
on their white paternity. It also placed a premium on Black female fertility.
Other colonies followed suit, and it became a codified practice that
children born to enslaved mothers would also be enslaved.

INCITING REVOLT

SAM (LIFE DATES UNKNOWN)

In 1680, Virginia's House of Burgesses passed "An Act for Preventing Negroes Insurrections," which made it illegal for an enslaved person to carry arms and to leave his master's property without a certificate of permission. It further noted, "the frequent meeting of considerable numbers of negroe slaves under pretence of feasts and burials [is] judged of dangerous consequence."[19] This statute reflects growing white fears of slave revolt—fears that intensified as the colony's Black population exploded and planters relied increasingly on enslaved Black labor. In 1660, Britain became officially involved in the transatlantic slave trade and the Royal African Company, chartered in 1672, provided a steady supply of captive Africans to British colonies in the Caribbean and North America. As their numbers increased on plantations throughout the Chesapeake, enslaved Black people began gathering when off-duty to practice their African traditions—such as feasts and burials—and, sometimes, to plan rebellions.[20]

White fear of slave insurrection was particularly strong in more sparsely settled regions of Virginia far from the colony's population centers along the James River. In 1687, Westmoreland County on the Potomac River became a hotspot of slave conspiracy and Sam, enslaved by the tobacco planter Richard Metcalfe, became a target of the authorities' punitive wrath. In October, a colonial official uncovered a "Negro Plott" to kill white colonists and he apprehended the suspected conspirators. Although the records have been lost, it is assumed that the suspects were executed. The Westmoreland Slave Plot prompted Governor Effingham (Francis Howard, fifth Baron Howard of Effingham), to issue a proclamation in which he repeated the terms of the 1680 statute and scolded slaveholders for "not restraining their Negroes from walking and rambling on broad on Satterdays and Sundays." Such permissiveness, he claimed, gave enslaved people the opportunity to

Enslaved man wearing a
punishment collar (detail),
plate from Jean-Baptiste
Debret, *Voyage Pittoresque
et Historique au Brésil*
(Paris: Firmin Didot Frères,
1834–1839).

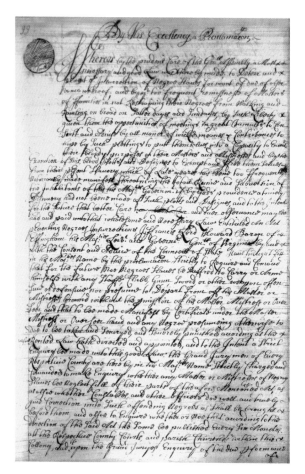

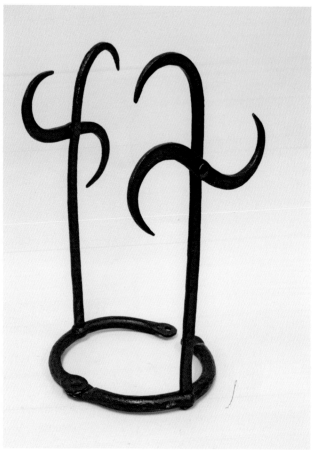

plan "all manner of wicked meanes and contrivances to hope by such plottings to . . . free themselves from their present slavery" (see fig.).

Sam's involvement in the 1687 plot is undocumented, but in the following year, the General Court convicted him of having "several times endeavoured to promote a Negro Insurreccon in this Colony." His punishment was harsh—authorities wanted to make an example of him to deter other would-be rebels. They sentenced Sam to be whipped and paraded around James City, where the court met, and then whipped again upon his return to Westmoreland County. In addition, they ordered "that hee have a strong Iron collar affixed about his neck with four spriggs which collar he is never to take or get off nor to goe off his master or masters plantacon during all the time he shall live," under penalty of death by hanging.[21] Sam's punishment collar was not only a constant source of physical discomfort, but also a conspicuous sign that white society considered him a troublemaker.

In subsequent decades, Virginia's colonial government repeatedly passed laws trying to restrict slave gatherings and travel off plantation—a clear indication of continued white fear of insurrection and of enduring Black desire for liberty.

[left] Proclamation by Governor Effingham (Francis Howard, fifth Baron Howard of Effingham), November 1687.
York County Deeds, Orders, Wills, 8, 1687–1691, Library of Virginia

[right] Punishment collar, date unknown.
African American Historical Society of Portsmouth

RISKING THE PLANTER'S WRATH

BAMBARA HARRY (ABOUT 1664–AFTER 1708) AND DINAH (1682–AFTER 1708)

The story of Bambara Harry and Dinah reflects power dynamics embedded in the system of slavery that, by the 18th century, was fully entrenched throughout the Chesapeake region. In this system, economic and political power was concentrated in the hands of a small number of landed elites, who built their fortunes off the labors of enslaved people. This ruling class controlled all the levers of government and used them to their benefit.[22]

Bambara Harry and Dinah were among the hundreds of people enslaved by Robert "King" Carter (1663–1732) of Lancaster County. Carter was the wealthiest planter and one of the most powerful men in colonial Virginia—hence his nickname "King." From Corotoman, his great estate on the Rappahannock River, he ran a hugely successful import-export business shipping tobacco, slaves, and other goods around the world, and he amassed land holdings totaling around 300,000 acres. Carter also served in Virginia's government in various positions, including speaker of the House of Burgesses and president of the governor's council.

In 1708, Bambara Harry and Dinah, who worked at Corotoman, tried to self-emancipate or run away. Their act of rebellion prompted Carter to seek redress from the law—and to make an example of them for his other slaves. On March 10, 1708, the Lancaster County Court issued the following authorization:

> Robert Carter Esq Complaining to this Court against two Incorrigible negroes of his named Bambara Harry & Dinah and praying the order of this Court for punishing the said negroes by dismembering them. It is therefore ordered that for the better reclaiming the said negroes & deterring others from the practices that said Robert Carter Esq have full power according to Law to

dismember the said negroes or either of them by cutting off their toes (see fig.).

The fact that the court labelled Bambara Harry and Dinah "incorrigible" and granted Carter permission to cut off their toes implies that one or both of them had previously attempted to escape. Slaveholders regularly disciplined their enslaved workers with whippings but reserved the more extreme measure of dismemberment for repeat "offenders." Carter used this punishment on several occasions, claiming "I have cured many a negro of running away by this means."[23] In the ruthless logic of slavery, amputating a person's toes would hamper their physical mobility—making it harder to run—but not their ability to work.

Bambara Harry and Dinah's ultimate fates are unknown. Their story—known only through this 1708 court record—underscores not just the brutality of slavery, but also the intense determination of enslaved people to be free. They were willing to risk amputation for liberty.

Ironically, Robert Carter III, "King" Carter's grandson who inherited his family's fortune and privilege, decided to gradually emancipate his more than 500 slaves beginning in 1791. This plan was the largest recorded emancipation by an individual slaveholder in U.S. history.

[above left] Enslaved couple escaping (detail), from Thomas Moran, *Slave Hunt, Dismal Swamp, Virginia*, 1861–1862, oil on canvas.
Philbrook Museum of Art, Tulsa, Oklahoma. Gift of Laura A. Clubb, 1947.8.44

[above right] Unidentified artist, *Robert "King" Carter,* about 1690–1726, oil on canvas.
Shirley Plantation, Charles City, Virginia

[right] "Carter & Negroes," entry (highlighted) from the Lancaster County Court Order Book, March 10, 1708.
Courtesy of Library of Virginia

Sheriff to cause to appear upon the Lands in difference in able Jury of presentable of the beverage such as are not any way related in Consanguinity or affinity & meet Mr. _____ Conway Survey'd on the Last Monday in Aprl or the next fair day & Survey & lay out the Land according to the most known ancient & reputed bounds of the same having regard to elder patents & such evidence as shall appear & if you find the ____ a Trespasser ye shall value damage & make report thereof to the next Cort und ye hands & Seals

Carter }
Cobley } Thomas Cobley servt to the Honoble Robert Carter Esqr confessing to this Court that he had absented himself from his sd masters service sixty four days It is therefore ordd Ct that ye he serve for the same one hundred & Eight days and forasmuch as it appeares to this Court that his sd master has Expended one hundred pounds of tobacco in the suit of the sd Thomas It is therefore ordered that he serve six weeks more after his time by Indenture Custome or ord of Court is Expired

Carter } & negros Robert Carter Esqr Complaining to this Court of two Incorrigible negros of his named Bambara Harry & Dinah and praying the ord of this Court for punishing the sd negros by dismembring them It is therefore ordered That for the better reclaiming the sd negros & determing others from ill practices That ye sd Robert Carter Esqr have full power acording to Law to dismember the sd negros or either of them by cutting of their toes

Rowden } Ordered that Jane Rowden be paid out of Wm Clinsons Estate in the hands of & sd Jno Aulterville the sum of three hundred pounds of tobacco &

Merridith } Ordered that Wm Merridith be paid out of the Estate of Wm Clinson in the & hands of sd Jno Thulterville Sixty six pounds of tobacco

Criss } Ordered that Criss a free negroe woman be pd out of the Estate of Wm & Clinson Decd in the hands of sd Jno Thulterville two hundred pounds of tobacco for funerall Charges

Gibson } Ordered that Robert Gibson doe pay unto sd Jno Thulterville ye Contents of & a Judgmt & Cost obtained by Wm Clinson in his life time agt ye sd Gibson with Cost alr Ext and it is like wise ordered that ye sd Jno Thulterville yield acct thereof to ye Court when thereunto required

Hamon } Judgmt is granted to Job Hamon Extor of the Last will & Testamt of Rd. wood
Pine }   decd agt Jno Pine for ye sum of six pound fourteen shills & four
23 July } pence due upon bala o sraty proved & oath deft & ordered to be forthwith
1708 }   paid with Cost alr Ext
No Deft }

         Mr Jno Pine enters mr Tho: Pheme his attorney

Dale & } Ordered that if Evident firms brought to this Court by James Dale agt Wm good
Goodridge } ridge deft in ye stead & place of Wm Baker be retrd for by a jeury att ye
              next Court

Dale &
Robinson } Idem

Gibron & } The action brought to this Court by Jno Thulterville agt Uriah Garton is Continued
Garton }   till next Court

Smith & } The action brought to this Court by Joseph Smith agt Robert Gibson is Continued
Gibson }   till next Court

Will Jack & } The action brought to this Court by Will & Jack two Eye Indians agt Capt Pinkar
Pinkard }   is dismt neither appearing

                    Present Capt Richd Ball

233

2
SLAVERY AT HIGH TIDE, 1775–1865

CHAPTER 2:
SLAVERY AT HIGH TIDE,
1775–1865

"We hold these truths to be self-evident, that all men are created equal, that they are endowed by their Creator with certain unalienable Rights, that among these are Life, Liberty and the pursuit of Happiness."
– Declaration of Independence, 1776[24]

The Foundational Paradox

One of the most difficult paradoxes of American history is the nation's foundation on both the ideal of liberty *and* the reality of slavery. George Washington and Thomas Jefferson—both elite Virginia planters and Founding Fathers—embody this fundamental contradiction. They devoted their lives to American liberty, while also holding hundreds of human beings in bondage. This chapter covers the period from the American Revolution (1775–1783) through the Civil War (1861–1865)—wars that, respectively, established the United States as a sovereign nation and nearly tore it asunder.

At the outbreak of the Revolutionary War, slavery existed in every one of the Thirteen Colonies, although at a significantly smaller scale in New England than in the Mid-Atlantic and South. Against this backdrop, America's leaders championed Enlightenment ideals of liberty, equality, and self-rule in their fight for independence from Britain and as the basis for the new republic. Debates over slavery animated the Constitutional Convention of 1787, which created the federal government and the U.S. Constitution. As Virginia delegate James Madison noted, "the real difference of interests lies not between the large and small but between the northern and southern states. The institution of slavery and its consequences form the line of discrimination."[25] One of the most contentious arguments involved whether to count slaves in the apportionment of congressional representatives, which is based on

Enslaved family at the Gaines House, Hanover Country, Virginia, 1862, photographed by G. H. Houghton.
Library of Congress

population. The resulting compromise counted an enslaved person as three-fifths of a person—a formula that gave Southern slaveholding states an advantage in national politics until the Civil War. This and other concessions to slavery ensured the ratification of the Constitution, but sowed the seeds of future division.

Reckoning with Slavery

Black Americans embraced revolutionary ideals to bolster their own demands for freedom and rights. These principles also inspired some white Americans to reconsider their thoughts on human bondage—as did growing moral condemnation of slavery from abolitionists and certain religious denominations, particularly Quakers. Between 1777 and 1804, all of the Northern states, except Delaware and Maryland, abolished slavery on an immediate or gradual basis. In Virginia, several prominent citizens called for an end to slavery, including St. George Tucker, a legal scholar and judge who unsuccessfully tried to get the legislature to consider his abolition proposal in 1796. Some slaveholders decided to manumit (emancipate) their enslaved laborers. The General Assembly made this process easier in 1782 by dropping the longstanding requirement for government permission. This led to a wave of manumissions that freed approximately 10,000 Black Virginians by 1806.[26]

Yet many Americans chose to maintain the system of human bondage. Slavery's supporters justified the institution with the specious claims of scientific racism. This pseudo-science asserted that the races were biologically distinct, therefore *un*equal, and that the white race was superior to all others. It also perpetuated racist stereotypes, including that Black people were unintelligent, animalistic, sexually promiscuous, and musically and athletically inclined. (Modern science has debunked claims of biological difference among the races—all humans share 99.9 percent of their DNA—nevertheless, the influence of scientific racism persists.)[27]

Apologists for slavery also promoted paternalism. According to this ideology, slavery was a beneficial system based on mutual obligations: slaveholders took care of enslaved people, whose purportedly childlike and imprudent nature made them incapable of doing so, in exchange for their labor and obedience. Many of slavery's defenders echoed George Fitzhugh of Virginia, who wrote that "the Negro slaves of the South are the happiest and, in some sense, the freest people in the world"—and better-off than wage workers in Northern factories—because they do not have to worry about life's necessities.[28] Paternalism not only denied the oppressive brutality of slavery, but it

Benjamin Henry Latrobe, *An Overseer Doing His Duty near Fredericksburg*, about 1798, watercolor on paper.
Courtesy of the Maryland Center for History and Culture, Item ID 1960.108.1.3.21.

was also belied by the rebellion of enslaved people and the success of free Black people in carving out meaningful lives.

The Growing Divide

Throughout this period, slavery became more deeply entrenched in Southern states—as well as in the nation's economy. It linked agricultural production in the South to banking and manufacturing industries in the North and drove the development of America's transportation and trade networks. In Virginia, the number of enslaved people exploded from approximately 292,000 in 1790 to 491,000 in 1860.[29] The vast majority of this enslaved population lived east of the Blue Ridge Mountains, in counties with large plantations and factories, maritime trades, and urban centers. Tobacco remained vital to the Commonwealth, even as its economy diversified with other crops and industries—all of which relied heavily on forced Black labor.

By the mid-19th century, Virginia's primary commodity and export, however, was *not* tobacco but slaves. The 1793 invention of the cotton gin fueled the rise of "King Cotton" across the Deep South, including in the new states of Alabama and Mississippi. As cotton production increased dramatically, so too did the demand for enslaved workers.

Map of the United States during the Civil War, 1861–1865

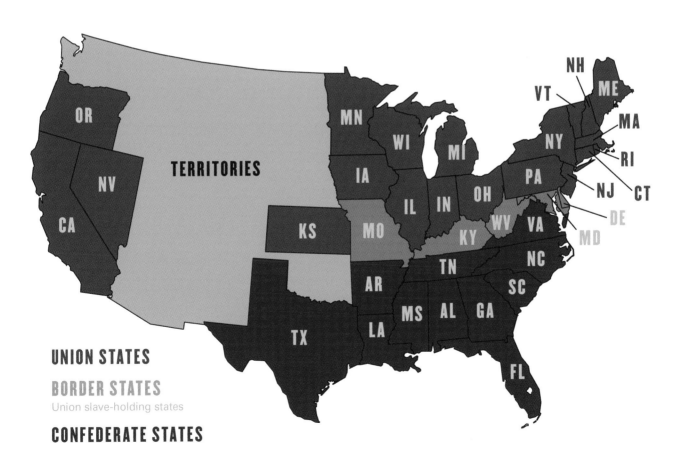

UNION STATES

BORDER STATES
Union slave-holding states

CONFEDERATE STATES

For slaveholders, enslaved people were valuable assets to be exploited for labor or sold for profit. After the 1808 federal ban on the importation of captive Africans, the domestic or internal slave trade ramped up. Virginia became the nation's largest supplier of enslaved workers, sending hundreds of thousands of Black people from the Upper to the Lower South (see "The Business of Slavery," p. 76). Virginia's government actively protected the institution of slavery against perceived threats. For instance, the General Assembly passed legislation in 1836 barring members of abolitionist organizations from entering the state.

Slavery also dominated national discourse and fostered a deepening divide between the more urban and industrial North and the heavily agricultural South. Westward expansion exacerbated this sectional rift. As the United States extended its boundaries across the continent—decimating and displacing Native peoples—the country's leaders fought bitterly over whether slavery should exist in new states. Congress struck the Missouri Compromise in 1820 and the Compromise of 1850 to maintain a balance of power between slave and free states, but the terms remained controversial (see entry on Anthony Burns, p. 80). In

Company E, 4th U.S. Colored Infantry, at Fort Lincoln, Washington, D.C., 1863–1865.
Library of Congress

the 1850s, growing animosity between pro- and antislavery factions made compromise over slavery increasingly impossible. For example, violent clashes erupted in the Kansas Territory in the wake of the Kansas-Nebraska Act (1854), which allowed settlers to determine its free or slave status, and in 1859 the militant abolitionist John Brown led an attempted revolt at Harpers Ferry (see entry on Dangerfield Newby, p. 84).

The final step on the road toward civil war was the 1860 election of President Abraham Lincoln, the Republican Party candidate opposed to the spread of slavery. In December, to preserve the institution, Southern slave states began seceding from the Union and formed the Confederate States of America. Its "cornerstone," according to Confederate vice president Alexander Stephens, "rests upon the great truth that the negro is not equal to the white man; that slavery, subordination to the superior race, is his natural and normal condition."[30] Confederates championed themselves as defenders of slavery and Southern sovereignty, while many Northerners viewed them as traitors to the United States.

Virginia seceded shortly after fighting broke out in South Carolina, when Confederate forces attacked the federal garrison at Fort Sumter on April 12, 1861. Most Virginia counties supported the Confederacy, but some political leaders, primarily from the northern and western regions of the state, remained loyal to the Union and formed West Virginia in 1863. Richmond became the Confederate capital, and Virginia would be a key battleground throughout the war.

When fighting began, nearly four million people were enslaved in the United States. For Black Americans this was a war for freedom, and they contributed to the war effort in various ways (see entry on Miles James, p. 87). Four years of bloody conflict led to the loss of as many as 750,000 lives. The costs were high, but so too were the stakes. Federal victory ultimately preserved the Union and ended 246 years of slavery in America.

REVOLUTIONARY CHOICES

RALPH HENRY (ABOUT 1754–AFTER 1793)
AND JAMES LAFAYETTE (ABOUT 1748–1830)

Black Virginians embraced the spirit of liberty that inspired America's fight for independence and applied it to their own struggle against slavery. During the Revolutionary War, enslaved people often chose sides—American or British—based on their own prospects for freedom from bondage.

In 1776, Ralph Henry of Gloucester County fled enslavement and cast his lot with the British.[31] He was likely motivated by the November 1775 proclamation issued by Lord Dunmore, Virginia's royal governor, who—in an effort to undermine patriot rebels by draining their workforce—offered freedom to enslaved men who fought for the British. "Dunmore's Proclamation" spurred a tidal wave of runaways in Virginia and, as word spread, throughout the colonies—more than 15,000 during the war.

Henry sailed to New York City with Dunmore and his troops and served with the Royal Artillery Division. He married Miney, an escaped slave from Philadelphia, and they had a daughter, Molly. In 1783, at the war's end, the Henry family was among the 3,000 so-called Black Loyalists who evacuated with defeated British forces and relocated to various parts of the British Empire. From New York, the Henrys went to Nova Scotia in Canada, where they endured privations and prejudice. In 1792—lured by the promise of Black self-rule and a better life—Henry emigrated to the new British colony of Sierra Leone in Africa. In 1793 (his last known appearance in the historical record), he was still fighting for liberty as one of eight leaders of a failed rebellion against British control.[32]

John Singleton Copley,
*Death of Major Peirson,
January 6, 1781* (detail),
1783, oil on canvas.
© Tate, London 2021

The Henry family (highlighted) in "The Book of Negroes," a ledger recording the Black Americans who evacuated New York City with the British Army, 1783.

The National Archives of the UK, ref. PRO30/55/100

Born into slavery in New Kent County, James Lafayette chose to support the patriot cause. In 1781, he obtained permission from his enslaver, William Armistead, to work as a spy for the Marquis de Lafayette, commander of the American forces in Virginia. Pretending to be a fugitive slave, James infiltrated British camps at Portsmouth and Yorktown. He carried messages to other spies behind enemy lines and secretly passed information back to Lafayette. The intelligence James gathered contributed to America's decisive victory at Yorktown in October 1781.

After the war, James petitioned the state for his freedom, describing how he "secretly conveyed enclosures from the Marquis into the Enemies lines of the most important kind" and "often at the peril of his life" (see fig.). Appealing to the legislators' patriotic spirit, he asked that "he may be granted that freedom which he flatters himself he has in some degree contributed to establish." The Marquis de Lafayette also provided a written testimonial lauding James's wartime service. In 1787,

[left] John B. Martin, *James Armistead Lafayette*, about 1824, oil on canvas.
The Valentine

[right] James Lafayette's petition for freedom, November 30, 1786.
Legislative Petitions of the General Assembly. Courtesy of Library of Virginia

the General Assembly granted him his freedom; years later, the state also gave him a pension. As a free man, James took Lafayette's last name and farmed forty acres in New Kent County.

Aligning themselves with different sides of the American Revolution, both Ralph Henry and James Lafayette ultimately succeeded in gaining their freedom. The risks that they took—the American army sometimes killed runaway slaves working for the enemy and both sides executed spies—underscore the depth of their common desire for liberty.

To the honorable the Speaker & gentlemen of the Genl. assembly,

The petition of James (a slave belonging to Will: armistead of New Kent county) humbly sheweth: That your petitioner persuaded of the just rights which all mankind have to freedom, notwithstanding his own state of bondage, with an honest desire to serve this country in its defence thereof, did, during the ravages of Lord Cornwallis thro' this state, by the permission of his master, enter into the service of the Marquiss Lafayette: That during the time of his serving the marquiss he often at the peril of his life found means to frequent the British camp, by which means he kept open a channel of the most useful communication to the army of the state: That at different times your petitioner conveyed inclosures, from the marquiss into the enemies lines, of the most important kind; the possession of which if discovered on him would have most certainly endangered the life of your petitioner: That he undertook & performed all commands with chearfulness & fidelity, in opposition to the persuasion & example of many thousands of his unfortunate condition. For proof of the above your petitioner begs leave to refer to certificate of the Marquiss Lafayette hereto annexed; & after taking his case as here stated into consideration he humbly intreats that he may be granted that freedom, which he flatters himself he has in some degree contributed to establish; & which he hopes always to prove himself worthy of: nor does he desire even this inestimable favor, unless his present master from whom he has experienced every thing which can make tolerable the state of slavery, shall be made adequate compensation for the loss of a valuable workman; which your petitioner humbly requests may be done & your petitioner shall ever pray &c ——

57

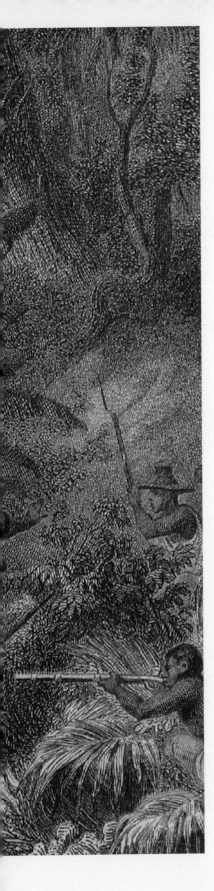

In the late 18th century, the Enlightenment ideals of freedom, independence, and democratic self-rule sparked revolutions around the Western hemisphere, including the:

- **American Revolution** (1775–1783)
- **French Revolution** (1789–1799)
- **Haitian Revolution** (1791–1804)
- **Wars for independence in Spain's American colonies** (1810s–1820s).

Enslaved Virginians also embraced the revolutionary spirit—most notably, Gabriel, a blacksmith who was inspired, in part, by the successful slave uprising in the French colony of Saint-Domingue, which established Haiti as a Black-led republic. In August 1800, Gabriel and other enslaved collaborators planned an insurrection that would begin in the Richmond area and spread through neighboring counties. As part of their plot, the rebels would kidnap Governor James Monroe and, in an allusion to Patrick Henry's famous speech during the American Revolution, march under a flag emblazoned "death or liberty."[33]

A torrential rainstorm and the authorities—who had been tipped off about the plan—thwarted the rebellion before it began. The state executed twenty-six conspirators, including Gabriel, but it could not suppress enslaved people's desire for liberty.

"Santo Domingo, the Capture of the Ravine-à-Couleuvres," illustration of the Haitian Revolution from Pierre Lanfrey, *The History of Napoleon the First* (4 vols.; London: Macmillan & Co., 1871–1879), ill. in vol. 2.
Rare Books and Special Collections, McGill University Library, Montreal

THE EMANCIPATOR

JANE MINOR (1790–AFTER 1859)

"I do . . . manumit, emancipate & set free"[34]

Throughout the history of American slavery, Virginia had the largest number of enslaved people of any colony or state. Yet not all Black Virginians lived in bondage. Free people of color made up more than 3 percent of the state's population in 1820 (the enslaved about 40 percent). Freedom, however, did *not* mean equality: free Black people still faced rampant discrimination as well as restricted civil rights. For instance, they could not serve on juries, testify against white people, or carry weapons without a special permit. Newly emancipated individuals were required to leave the state after one year unless they obtained authorization to stay. The majority of Virginia's free Black population lived in cities where they found a degree of safety and solidarity. In these communities, free individuals often intermingled with and helped urban slaves who were hired out to labor outside the enslaver's household.

Jane Minor, also known as Jensey Snow, was an important figure in antebellum Petersburg's Black community. Born into slavery, she earned her freedom and local fame through her talents as a healer. Her enslaver, Dr. Benjamin Harrison May, might have trained her and used her as an assistant in his own practice because he was partially blind. In 1825, May emancipated Minor for her "general good character and conduct" and for her service during an epidemic, noting that she performed

> several acts of extraordinary merit . . . in nursing & at the imminent risk of her own health & safety, exercising the most unexampled patience and attention in watching over the sick beds of several individuals of this town.[35]

John Donaghy, "The Great Battle between the Board of Health and the Marketmen" (detail), 1873, illustration.
Courtesy of VCU Libraries, Tompkins-McCaw Library Special Collections & Archives

I Jane Minor, otherwise called Jersey Snow, have this day emancipated & set free & I do by these presents emancipat, manumit & set free five mulatto children slaves belonging to me by name Daniel, George, Martha Rebecca, Arena, and Alfred (otherwise called Daniel George, Martha R., Arena and Alfred Smith) and I do hereby declare the said slaves to be henceforth entitled to all the rights & privileges of free persons with which it is in my power to invest them; they being the children of Emily Smith whom I purchased this day of David May as will appear by his Bill of sale hereto annexed. In Testimony whereof I have hereto set my hand & affixed my seal the 31st day of July 1840.

Witness }
James May }
David May }

Jane [her mark] Minor [seal]

I David May for & in consideration of the sum of fifteen hundred dollars by Jane Minor (otherwise called Jersey Snow) to me in hand paid the receipt whereof is hereby acknowledged have bargained & sold & I do by these presents bargain & sell unto the said Jane Minor (otherwise called Jersey Snow) a mulatto woman slave by name Emily (otherwise called Emily Smith) and her five children, namely, Daniel, George, Martha Rebecca, Arena, and Alfred; the right & title to which said slaves I hereby warrant & defend unto the said Jane Minor (otherwise called Jersey Snow) against the claims of all persons whatsoever. In testimony whereof I have hereto set my hand & affixed my seal this 31st day of July A.D. 1840.

David May [seal]

At a Hustings Court held for the Town of Petersburg at the Court house on the 17th day of December A.D. 1840

A deed of emancipation from Jane Minor to Daniel Smith and others having been partly proved in the said Court on the 22nd day of August 1840 by the oath of David May one of the witnesses thereto was this day fully proved by the oath of James May the other witness thereto and together with the bill of sale annexed ordered to be recorded

Exam'd }   Teste

D. M. Bernard CC

Manumission deed issued by Jane Minor for Emily Smith and her children, Petersburg Hustings Court Deed Book 11, July 31, 1840.
Petersburg City Court

As a free woman, Minor continued tending the sick, both white and Black. About a dozen extant receipts provide a fragmentary glimpse of her practice, with her fees ranging from $1 to $10 for bloodletting (cupping and leeching), and $6 to more than $60 for nursing a patient through his last illness. This "well known nurse" also received occasional mentions in the local newspaper for her medical exploits.[36]

Perhaps Minor's most heroic work was as an emancipator. Between 1838 and 1842, she freed or manumitted sixteen women and children from enslavement. For example, in July 1840, she "emancipated and set free" Emily Smith and her five children after purchasing them for $1,500—about $44,000 today (see fig.). That same month, Minor also

Cupping jar used for bloodletting, late 18th century.
The Valentine

manumitted a fellow nurse, "a mulatto woman slave named Phebe [Jackson] who has resided in Petersburg for some years past & who has been employed generally in nursing sick people & leeching, &c."[37] Minor could have trained Phebe in the healing arts, suggesting the kind of collaborative relationships upon which Black communities relied. To fund her emancipation efforts, Minor likely used her own earnings along with money provided by the families she helped.

Through a combination of skill, social networks, and commitment to serving others, Jane Minor found ways to improve the lives of Black people and counteract the racial oppression of antebellum Virginia.

EMIGRATING TO AFRICA

LOTT CARY (1780–1828)

"I wish to go to a country where I shall be estimated by merits, not by my complexion."[38]

Rev. Lott Cary, illustration from Carter G. Woodson, *History of the Negro Church* (Washington, D.C.: Associated Publishers, 1921).
VMHC

In the post-Revolutionary period, the growing number of free Black Americans—more than 30,000 in Virginia in 1810—threatened white supremacy and the institution of slavery. Free people of color demanded the rights of citizenship and presented what slaveholders feared was a dangerous example to the enslaved populace. Founded in 1816, the American Colonization Society (ACS) proposed one solution to these tensions: send free Black Americans to Africa. An unlikely coalition of Black people, abolitionists, and proslavery whites supported the colonization movement—united in part by a shared belief that the two races could never live in harmony. Prominent Virginians, including U.S. Chief Justice of the Supreme Court John Marshall and Presidents James Madison and James Monroe were all involved in the ACS.[39]

Lott Cary, a former slave and Baptist minister, was a leading Black proponent of African emigration and a "founding father" of the new colony of Liberia. Born in Charles City County, he worked in Richmond's tobacco factories as a hired slave. Through hard work and hustle—including earning bonuses and gathering unused scraps of tobacco to sell—Cary saved enough money to purchase his freedom. In the 1810s, he became active as a Baptist lay preacher and missionary.

In 1821, Cary and a small group of free Black Richmonders set sail for the West Coast of Africa under the auspices of the ACS. Over the next few years, he led the settlement of Liberia—deploying his entrepreneurial acumen to acquire land, build the capital of Monrovia, establish a school and church, and create a trading company to exchange local products for supplies. He also wrested more control of the colony from the ACS's white agent and became vice agent in 1826.

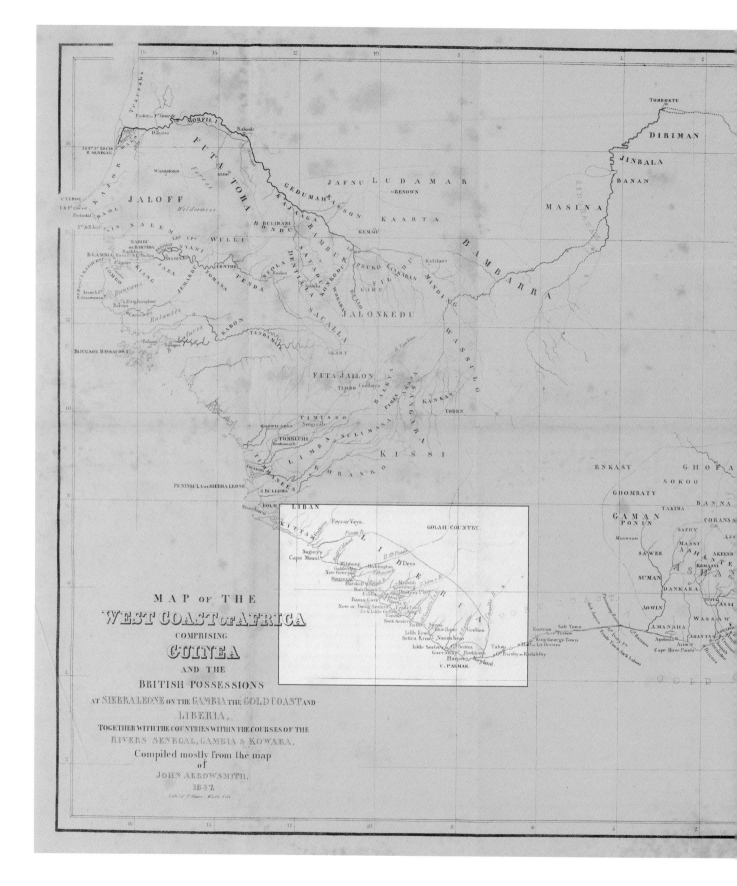

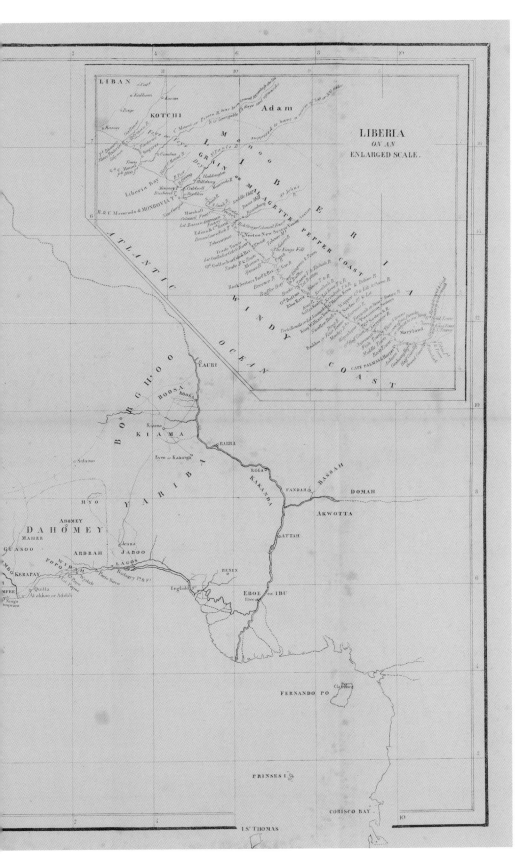

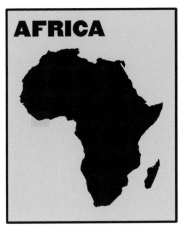

Liberia (highlighted), from John Arrowsmith, *Map of the West Coast of Africa* (Washington, D.C.: P. Haas, 1842).

VMHC

The early emigrants faced hostile conditions, including disease, crop failures, and armed conflict with native inhabitants. Nevertheless, Cary remained committed to Liberia's success. In one of his reports to the Richmond auxiliary of the ACS, he noted, "We have a good country . . . why not send out the people of colour as fast as possible" (see fig.). He also argued that emigration offered Black Americans new opportunities as well as freedom from poverty and prejudice.[40] Cary died in 1828 from a gunpowder accident. His efforts laid the groundwork for Liberia to become, in 1847, an independent republic with another Black Virginian, Joseph Jenkins Roberts, as its first president.

Despite Cary's rosy pronouncements, the colonization movement was controversial among Black Americans. The *Colored American* newspaper, for example, argued, "This Country is Our Only Home. It is our duty and privilege to claim an equal place among the American people."[41] But for the 15,000 free Black people who emigrated to Liberia between 1821 and 1860, leaving the United States—and its entrenched racism—seemed the only viable option for a better life.[42] Ironically, settlers reproduced certain American inequities, including forcing native inhabitants to work and denying them rights. The civil strife that has plagued modern Liberia is rooted in these early tensions between American- and African-born Liberians.

Letter from Lott Cary, Monrovia, Liberia, to Benjamin Brand, Richmond, April 3, 1825.
VMHC

Spirituality and the church served a vital role in Black communities throughout slavery and beyond. Many Africans forcibly transported to America became Christians, finding hope and comfort amid their earthly sufferings in the Christian paradigm of Jesus's martyrdom and the promise of a heavenly reward. Other enslaved Africans retained the diverse faiths of their homelands, including Islam. Religious practices nurtured the soul and fostered Black pride in the face of the dehumanizing effects of slavery and segregation. Passed down through the generations, such practices also helped preserve African traditions through music, funeral customs, and call-and-response forms of worship. Religious meetings—whether secret gatherings in the woods or church congregations—became crucibles for collective activism.

Religion also played a major role in debates over slavery. Antislavery advocates, including abolitionists, Quakers, and others, condemned the evils of slavery and its corruptive effects on enslavers, while also celebrating Black humanity. By contrast, slaveholders and their supporters justified slavery with theological arguments, including claims that slavery exists in the Bible and that slaveholders bring salvation to a "heathen" race by converting enslaved people to Christianity. Enslavers also used the Bible to control slaves, citing Paul's Epistles, which command obedience to one's master.

[above] John Antrobus, *A Plantation Burial*, 1860, oil on canvas.
The Historic New Orleans Collection, The L. Kemper and Leila Moore Williams Founders Collection, 1960.46

SEEKING FREEDOM BY THE SWORD

NAT TURNER (1800–1830)

In August 1831, Nat Turner led the bloodiest slave revolt in American history in Southampton County. This insurrection sent shockwaves across the nation that reverberated for decades. An enslaved preacher and self-proclaimed prophet, Turner believed he was "ordained for some great purpose in the hands of the Almighty"—to end the evils of slavery.[43] In the late 1820s, he and four trusted colleagues—Henry Porter, Hark Moore, Nelson Edwards, and Sam Francis—began secretly meeting in the woods to plot a revolt. Willing to die for his cause, Turner envisioned an apocalyptic conflict: "I saw white spirits and black spirits engaged in battle, and the sun was darkened—the thunder rolled in the Heavens, and blood flowed in streams."[44] He also embraced the political symbolism of starting the insurrection on the Fourth of July. (Turner changed his dates based on astronomical events that he saw as signs from God.)

The revolt began on the night of August 21, 1831, at the home of Turner's enslaver, Joseph Travis. Using the element of surprise, the rebels slayed the family and then moved on to neighboring farms, killing white inhabitants—men, women, and children. They also gathered weapons and valuables, and recruited "soldiers" from among the enslaved. Turner's force grew to about forty men. As word of the attacks spread, the local white population mounted a defense and state militia rushed to the area. They quashed the insurrection about eighteen hours after it had started. Fifty-five white people lay dead.

The bloodshed continued. Throughout Southampton County and beyond, white vigilantes sought revenge by torturing and terrorizing Black communities and killing about forty people. One newspaper noted that this retaliatory violence was "hardly inferior in barbarity to the atrocities of the insurgents."[45] Turner eluded capture until October 31 by hiding out in the woods. The Commonwealth tried thirty-one of the

"Horrid Massacre in Virginia," broadside about Nat Turner's revolt, 1831.
VMHC

HORRID MASSACRE IN VIRGINIA.

The Scenes which the above Plate is designed to represent, are---Figure 1. a Mother intreating for the lives of her children.
---2. Mr. Travis, cruelly murdered by his own Slaves.---3. Mr. Barrow, who bravely defended himself until his wife escaped.
----4. A company of mounted Dragoons in pursuit of the Blacks.

Just Published, an Authentic and Interesting

NARRATIVE

OF THE

TRAGICAL SCENE

Which was witnessed in Southampton county (Virginia) on Monday the 22d of August last, when FIFTY FIVE of its inhabitants (mostly women and children) were inhumanly massacred by the Blacks!

Short and imperfect sketches of the horrid massacre above mentioned have appeared in the public Journals, but the public are now presented with every particular relative thereto, communicated by those who were eye witnesses of the bloody scene, and confirmed by the confessions of several of the Blacks while under sentence of death.

A more shocking instance of human butchery has seldom occurred in any country, and never before in this—the merciless wretches carried destruction to every white person they found in the houses, whether the hoary head, the lovely virgin, or the sleeping infant in the cradle! they spared none !—a widow (Mrs. Whitehead) and her 10 children were murdered in one house ! among the slain on that fatal night, was an amiable young lady but 17 years of age, who the day following was to have been united in marriage to a young gentleman of North-Carolina, who had left home the evening preceding with the expectation of conveying there the succeeding day the object of his affections ! but, alas ! how sad was his disappointment ! he was the third person who entered the house after the horrid massacre, to witness the mangled remains of her whom he was so shortly to espouse ! The Blacks after having completed their work of death, attempted to evade the pursuit of those who had collected to oppose them, by secreting themselves in a neighboring swamp, to the borders of which they were pursued by a company of mounted dragoons. Of the fifty five slain nearly two thirds of the number were children, not exceeding twelve years of age ! and it was truly a melancholly scene (as was observed to the writer by one who witnessed it) to behold on the day of their interment so great a number of coffins collected, surrounded by the weeping relatives !

While the friends of humanity however or wherever situated. cannot but sincerely and deeply lament the awful destruction of so many innocent lives, yet, the humane and philanthopic citizens of New-England, and of the middle States, cannot feel too thankful for the repose and peace of conscience which they enjoy, by wisely and humanely abolishing laws dooming a free born fellow being (without fault or crime) to perpetual bondage !---an example truly worthy of imitation by our brethren at the South.

The Narrative (which contains every important particular relating to the horrid massacre) is afforded for the trifling sum of 12 1-2 Cents.
☞ This paper left for perusal, and to be returned when called for.

"Nat Turner and His
Confederates in Council,"
illustration from Orville J.
Victor, *History of American
Conspiracies* (New York:
James D. Torrey, 1863).
Schomburg Center for Research in
Black Culture, The New York Public
Library, 1229308

rebels. Ultimately, all the *Creole* captives except for five who chose to remain onboard and two rebels who died in prison gained their freedom.

The revolt's success was the result of a well-planned and disciplined operation, combined with the determination to be free. Plotting might have begun in a Richmond slave jail, where Madison Washington and several of his collaborators were held while awaiting transport. Washington worked as a cook aboard the ship, a post that allowed him to observe the crew's movements and to communicate with other enslaved passengers. The rebels knew that getting to British soil would give them a chance at liberty—knowledge of international law likely gained from recent freedom cases involving the slave ships *Amistad* (1839) and *Hermosa* (1840).

Widely reported in the press, the *Creole* revolt polarized the nation. Slaveholders fumed, while abolitionists rejoiced. This incident also strained Anglo-American diplomatic relations over the issues of slaveholders' property rights and British interference in American mercantile activity. Although Madison Washington disappeared from the historical record, he became a legend in antislavery literature as "the leader of the 'Immortal Nineteen'" who dealt a great blow to the institution of slavery.[49]

1860

$3.7 TRILLION
Value of enslaved people

$1.1 TRILLION
Value of all U.S. manufacturing

$500 MILLION
Value of all U.S. banks

OVER $10 TRILLION
Estimated value of labor provided by enslaved people between 1619 and 1865

Slavery was deeply entwined in the political, social, and—especially—the economic fabric of the United States. Enslaved people helped build the nation through their labors and through the wealth they brought to slaveholders and industries tied to the manufacture, transport, and sale of slave-harvested products, such as tobacco and cotton.

The internal or domestic slave trade was also a big business, especially in Virginia, which had a large enslaved population and two of the largest slave markets in antebellum America in Richmond and Alexandria. The Commonwealth was also the largest supplier of enslaved labor to other slave states—selling an estimated 350,000 individuals "Down South" between 1820 and 1860.[50]

In 1860, there were nearly four million enslaved Black people in the United States. This graph shows their paramount economic impact, in today's dollars, on the U.S. economy.[51]

The human costs of slavery are incalculable. They include the toll of physical and psychological torture and the trauma of family separation for one in three enslaved children and one in five married couples.

Lefevre Cranstone, *Slave Auction in Virginia*, 1860–1861, oil on canvas.
VMHC

INGENIOUS ESCAPE

HENRY "BOX" BROWN (1815/16–1897)

Since slavery began in Virginia, enslaved individuals sought their liberty by running away or self-emancipating. These hopeful freedom seekers faced numerous obstacles in the form of slave patrols, unfamiliar terrain, and lack of provisions during their journey, as well as retribution against their loved ones and harsh punishment if caught. Yet for many, the risk was worth the reward.

In 1849, Henry Brown made one of the most sensational and ingenious escapes from slavery. Born in Louisa County, he was sent to Richmond as a young man to work in a tobacco factory. In 1848, his wife Nancy and their children were sold to a slaveholder in North Carolina. For Brown, family separation was a "kind of torture [that] is a thousand fold more cruel and barbarous than the use of the lash."[52] Powerless to stop the sale, he walked beside Nancy and their children for four miles as they were marched out of Richmond in a slave coffle. He never saw them again.

The loss of his family spurred Brown's determination to escape slavery, or die trying. He hatched the idea of shipping himself like dry goods to a free state—an ironic twist on a slave's legal status as property. Two men with links to the Underground Railroad—James Caesar Anthony Smith, a free person of color, and Samuel A. Smith, a white shoemaker (no relation)—helped Brown with his plan. On March 29, 1849, they sealed him in a wooden crate measuring 3 feet long by 2½ feet wide by 2 feet deep and drilled with some air holes, and they forwarded it to Philadelphia.

Crammed into this box, Brown traveled by steamboat, wagon, and train, enduring physical agony and rough handling by cargo workers. Stuck upside-down at several points, he "felt my eyes swelling as if they would burst from their sockets; and the veins on my temples were dreadfully distended with pressure of blood upon my head."[53]

[above] Samuel W. Rowse, *The Resurrection of Henry Box Brown at Philadelphia*, 1850, lithograph.
VMHC

[left] Lewis Miller, *Slave Trader, Sold to Tennessee*, about 1853, watercolor and ink on paper.
The Colonial Williamsburg Foundation. Gift of Dr. and Mrs. Richard M. Kain in memory of George Hay Kain

He also passed out. After twenty-seven hours and 350 miles, the crate arrived at its destination—the office of the Pennsylvania Anti-Slavery Society, a major hub of the Underground Railroad. Miraculously, Brown survived his journey.

Upon gaining his freedom, he adopted the nickname "Box" and became a celebrity within abolitionist circles. Brown's daring escape was the subject of a ghost-written narrative (1849) and of the performances he gave to antislavery groups around the Northeast. He described his experience in religious terms, as a resurrection from death in bondage to life in liberty. "Certainly the deliverance of Moses, from destruction on the Nile," he wrote, "was scarcely more marvelous than was the deliverance of Mr. Henry Box Brown from the horrors of slavery."[54] Following the passage of the Fugitive Slave Act in 1850, he fled the United States to avoid recapture and continued his work as an abolitionist and entertainer in England, then Canada.

A powerful testimony of courage and ingenuity, Henry "Box" Brown's story served also to underscore the depth of enslaved people's desire for freedom and to refute slaveholders' claims that slaves were content with their lot.

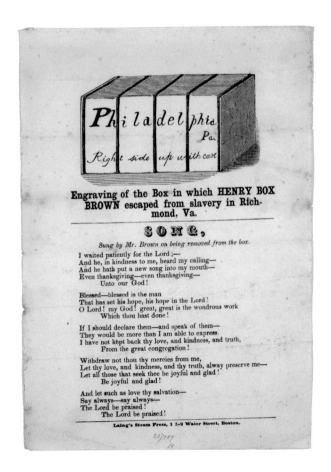

"Engraving of the box in which Henry Box Brown escaped from slavery in Richmond, Va. Song, sung by Mr. Brown on being removed from the box," broadside, 1850.

Library of Congress

ABOLITIONIST CAUSE CÉLÈBRE

ANTHONY BURNS (1834–1862)

I n 1854, Anthony Burns became a prominent test case of the Fugitive Slave Act and a lightning rod in the national debate over slavery. This controversial law was part of the Compromise of 1850, passed by the U.S. Congress to avert a sectional crisis over slavery. As originally written, the Constitution stated that "no person held to service or labor" would be released from bondage upon escaping to a free state. A 1793 fugitive slave law allowed slaveholders and their agents to travel across state lines to recapture so-called fugitives, but Northern states regularly resisted such efforts.

The Fugitive Slave Act of 1850 strengthened the existing law by giving the federal government powers of enforcement and by compelling Northerners to assist in the recovery of runaways. It privileged slaveholders' "property" rights over the rights of free states. This new act enraged antislavery factions and sent a chill through Black communities in the North that had long been a refuge for escaped slaves. Within its first three months, more than 3,000 Black Americans moved to Canada to avoid recapture.[55]

Born enslaved in Stafford County, Anthony Burns escaped from Richmond to Boston by stowing away on a ship in early 1854. His enslaver, Charles Suttle, discovered his location and traveled to Massachusetts to return him to slavery. In May, Suttle had Burns arrested and jailed at the Boston courthouse to await a trial authorizing his rendition.

Upon Burns's capture, Boston's large, interracial abolitionist community swung into action. They held a large protest meeting that culminated with a crowd swarming the courthouse to rescue Burns (see fig.). In 1851, abolitionist activists had broken

One of two checks used for the purchase of Anthony Burns, issued by City Bank, Boston, February 22, 1855.

Collection of Massachusetts Historical Society

[above left] "A Man Kidnapped!" poster advertising a meeting to help Anthony Burns after his recapture in Boston, May 26, 1854.
Boston Public Library, Rare Books Department

[above right] Anthony Burns, about 1855, printed by R. M. Edwards.
Library of Congress

Shadrach Minkins, another escaped Virginian, out of the same jail then transported him secretly to safety in Canada. This time, the authorities were better prepared and foiled the attempt, although one guard was killed in the melee.

Burns, who was represented by an abolitionist lawyer, lost his case. A particularly damning piece of evidence was the report of an exchange between Burns and Suttle when they met in Boston: "Haven't I always treated you well, Tony?" Suttle asked, "Haven't I always given you money when you needed?" Burns replied, "You have always given me 12 and one-half cents once a year."[56] The judge took this conversation as proof of Burns's enslavement and ordered him returned to bondage.

On June 1, authorities escorted Burns under military guard to a ship bound for Virginia. For several months, he languished in Richmond's infamous Lumpkin's slave jail awaiting sale to a new owner. Boston abolitionists continued fighting on his behalf and raised $1,300 to purchase Burns's freedom (see fig.). As a free man, he studied for the ministry at Oberlin College in Ohio and later moved to Canada.

Even though Southerners rejoiced in the successful enforcement of the Fugitive Slave Act, the depth of Northern resistance caused great concern. Burns's case galvanized abolitionists and intensified the activities of the Underground Railroad. He was the last person from New England remanded back to slavery under this law.[57]

ENDURING ENSLAVEMENT

SARAH CALWELL (1834–AFTER 1863)

For enslaved people trying to self-emancipate (run away) or lead an insurrection, the odds of success were very slim given the deeply entrenched systems at the local, state, and national level designed to keep them in bondage. The vast majority of enslaved individuals rebelled in safer and subtler ways, such as by working slowly, feigning illness, or breaking tools. And they persevered.

Sarah Calwell's story is typical of that of the hundreds of thousands of Black Americans who endured slavery—largely in obscurity—in antebellum Virginia. It is a fragmentary story, one told only through the records of her enslaver, not in her own voice. Yet, despite these archival silences, we can imagine a life marked by backbreaking labor and strict discipline, family love and separation, and hopes for a better future.

Calwell first appears in the historical record in October 1856, when Dr. Richard Eppes purchased the twenty-two-year-old from John D. Ragland of Petersburg. Described as an "excellent laundress," she was pregnant and gave birth to her daughter Elinora a few weeks later. Her laundry skills and her impending motherhood—proof of her fertility—contributed to the high sale price of $1,100.[58]

Eppes, scion of a long-established planter family, enslaved nearly 130 people and owned more than 2,200 acres of land around City Point and Hopewell. Calwell worked in the kitchen-laundry outbuilding of his main estate, Appomattox Manor. She toiled from sunrise to sunset, six days a week—washing, ironing, and mending clothing and linens for Eppes's large family and plantation operations. Her life was governed by his systematic approach to slave management. Eppes described his disciplinary philosophy using a biblical proverb: "'Spare the rod you spoil the child' is my best experience." His "Code of Laws," which he read aloud to his enslaved workforce every New Year's Day, outlines his rules about obedience, cleanliness, stealing, traveling off the plantation,

Thimbles found in archaeological excavations of the kitchen-laundry building of Appomattox Manor, 19th century.
Courtesy of Petersburg National Battlefield, PETE 11641

[above left] *A Southern Laundry*, about 1900, unidentified illustration.
VMHC, Photo Files

[above right] Richard Eppes, "Code of Laws for Island Plantation," about 1857.
VMHC, Gift of Elise Eppes Cutchin

and other behaviors, as well as the punishments for offenses—usually "stripes" (lashings with a whip) or reduced rations (see fig.).[59]

Calwell and her daughter lived apart from her husband, William, who was enslaved by Oliver Hamilton of Petersburg. The frequency of their visits is unknown, but they were willing to risk permanent separation for a chance at William's freedom. In 1858, he was one of five slaves captured while trying to escape on board the schooner *Keziah*. Authorities returned the "fugitives" to their slaveholders and sentenced the ship's captain—William Baylis of Delaware, a regular conductor on the Underground Railroad—to forty years in prison.

In 1862 as federal troops advanced toward City Point, the vast majority of Eppes's enslaved laborers fled seeking freedom across Union lines. Perhaps deterred by her husband's failed escape attempt, Sarah Calwell remained with the Eppes family when they evacuated to Petersburg. (Strategically located at the confluence of the James and Appomattox Rivers, the manor house at City Point became General Ulysses S. Grant's headquarters.) The fates of Sarah, William, and Elinora are unknown.

SOLDIER IN JOHN BROWN'S RAID

DANGERFIELD NEWBY (ABOUT 1820–1859)

"I . . . am now quite certain that the crimes of this guilty land will never be purged away but with blood."
– John Brown, 1859[60]

As the national divide between pro- and antislavery factions and between Southern slave states and free Northern ones deepened in the mid-19th century, some militant abolitionists like John Brown grew convinced that violent conflict was the only way to end slavery. In 1857, Brown began planning a slave insurrection that would begin in Harpers Ferry, Virginia (present-day West Virginia) and spread throughout the South. He spent two years assembling financial support and weapons—including 950 pikes commissioned from a Connecticut foundry—and raising a small army (see fig.).

Dangerfield Newby was one of five Black men in Brown's army. Born into slavery in Culpeper County, he was the son of a white father and enslaved mother who gained his freedom when the family moved to Ohio in 1858. The following year, Newby was back in the Shenandoah Valley trying to purchase the freedom of his enslaved wife, Harriet Newby, and their children. The family's plight was growing desperate, as Harriet expressed in an August 1859 letter to her husband:

> I want you to buy me as soon as possible for if you do not get me somebody else will . . . it is said Master is in want of money. If so I know not what time he may sell me and then all my bright hopes of the future are blasted.[61]

Unable to raise enough money to free his wife and children and fearing their sale Down South, Dangerfield Newby joined Brown's army. For him, the cause was deeply personal.

[above] Dangerfield Newby, about 1855.
Library of Congress

[left] Pike made for John Brown's planned slave revolt at Harpers Ferry, by Charles Blair foundry, Collinsville, Connecticut, 1859.
VMHC

Jacob Lawrence, *John Brown held Harpers Ferry for 12 hours. His defeat was a few hours off*, 1977, screenprint on wove paper, from *The Legend of John Brown* series, 1977.

Virginia Museum of Fine Arts, Richmond J. Harwood and Louise B. Cochrane Fund and partial gift of Derrick Johnson in honor of his grandson, Mark Devon Johnson, on the occasion of VMFA's 75th anniversary

On the night of October 16, 1859, Brown and his men began their raid on the federal armory at Harpers Ferry. They planned to seize the arsenal to supply weapons to the enslaved men who would rise up in revolt. Newby was fatally shot on the first day of fighting—the first of Brown's raiders to fall. Osborne Anderson, the only Black collaborator to survive, described Newby as "a brave fellow" and a martyr for freedom.[62] By October 18, the local militia and U.S. marines that had converged on the site quashed the rebellion. Brown's forces had killed five people; he and six of his men were captured, ten were dead, and five escaped. The Commonwealth of Virginia executed Brown and the other captives for murder, treason, and inciting slave insurrection. Newby's wife and children were sold to a slaveholder in Louisiana.

The raid at Harpers Ferry enflamed the sectional crisis over slavery, prompting many Americans to conclude that armed conflict was inevitable. As Frederick Douglass stated: "If John Brown did not end the war that ended slavery, he did, at least, begin the war that ended slavery."[63] Views on Brown as a martyr or madman remain as divided today as they were in the aftermath of the raid.

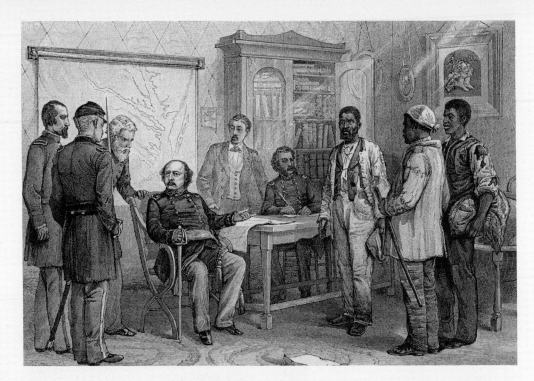

[above] "General Butler Refusing to Return Escaped Slaves Known as Contrabands," illustration from William Cullen Bryant and Sydney Howard Gay, *A Popular History of the United States*, vol. 4 (New York: Charles Scribner's Sons, 1880).
Wallach Division Picture Collection, The New York Public Library

[left] Edwin Forbes, *Coming into the Line, or Contrabands Approaching the Union Lines near Culpeper Court House, November 8, 1863*, 1876, engraving.
VMHC

In May 1861, three enslaved men who were being used to build a Confederate battery in Hampton Roads—Frank Baker, Sheppard Mallory, and James Townsend—escaped to the U.S. military garrison Fort Monroe. When a Confederate officer came to reclaim them, the fort's commander, Major General Benjamin Butler, refused to return the men. He considered them "contraband of war"—property used for enemy purposes. A few months later, Congress adopted this as federal policy to deprive the Confederacy of its labor force. As word of this policy spread, enslaved people ran away in throngs to Fort Monroe, which became known as "Freedom's Fortress," and other Union strongholds. During the Civil War, nearly 500,000 enslaved people sought refuge behind federal lines, especially in Virginia, one of the primary theaters of the war. For these individuals, becoming a "contraband" was their first step toward emancipation. Many also contributed to the Union war effort.

"A MODEL SOLDIER"

MILES JAMES (1829–1871)

Army of the James Medal ("Butler Medal"), commissioned for USCT soldiers who fought at the battle of New Market Heights, 1864.

Courtesy of American Numismatic Society

A t the outset of the Civil War, U.S. officials debated enlisting Black men in the military. Some doubted their fighting capabilities, while others—including President Lincoln—feared alienating slaveholding states that remained loyal to the Union. In 1863, facing growing pressure from advocates and in need of men, the federal government finally authorized the use of Black soldiers and created the U.S. Colored Troops (USCT).

Free Black men and escaped slaves or "contrabands" embraced the opportunity to fight for the Union cause. Ultimately, about 178,000 Black men enlisted in the U.S. Army and 19,000 in the Navy. They served honorably, despite facing pervasive discrimination. For example, USCT regiments were segregated and commanded by white officers, and Black soldiers initially received lower wages than white troops—$10 per month compared to $13—until Congress equalized pay in 1864. They were also subject to added risks if captured: Confederates regularly executed or enslaved Black soldiers rather than treat them as prisoners of war.[64]

Miles James embodied the courage, determination, and sacrifice of the USCT. From Princess Anne County (today Virginia Beach), he was likely an escaped slave when he enlisted in the 36th Infantry, USCT, in November 1863. His military talents earned him promotion to corporal the following February. Stationed around Virginia, the 36th guarded prisoners of war, went on raids to liberate enslaved people, and fought in various battles. The regiment particularly distinguished itself during the bloody battle of New Market Heights on September 29, 1864, a federal offensive intended to weaken Confederate defenses around Richmond. It was also a chance for Black soldiers to prove their mettle. A brigade of USCT, including James's 36th regiment, charged up a bluff into the well-entrenched Confederate army. They met a heavy barrage of bullets—and suffered heavy casualties—yet ultimately broke through

[left] Letter from Col. Alonzo Draper to the Surgeon in Charge at the United States General Hospital, Fort Monroe, February 4, 1865.
National Archives, Records of the Adjutant General's Office

[right] Thomas Waterman Wood, *A Bit of War History: The Recruit*, 1866, oil on canvas.
The Metropolitan Museum of Art, Gift of Charles Stewart Smith, 1884

enemy lines. During the fighting, Corporal James was shot in the arm, but he continued to fight with his one good arm and spur his comrades on to victory.

The USCT garnered widespread praise for their valiant performance at New Market Heights, winning over skeptics who doubted their abilities. Even a Confederate soldier acknowledged that "no troops up to that time had fought us with more bravery than did those Negroes."[65] For his heroic actions, Miles James became one of only twenty-five Black recipients of the Medal of Honor from the Civil War; he also earned promotion to sergeant.

James lost his arm—it had to be amputated—but not his commitment to the Union cause. He successfully petitioned to remain on active duty in his regiment's provost guard (military police). His brigade commander, Colonel Alonzo Draper, wrote in support of James's petition: "He is one of the bravest men I ever saw; and is in every respect a model soldier. He is worth more with his single arm, than half a dozen ordinary men" (see fig.). The contributions of Black soldiers like Miles James helped end the Civil War and American slavery.

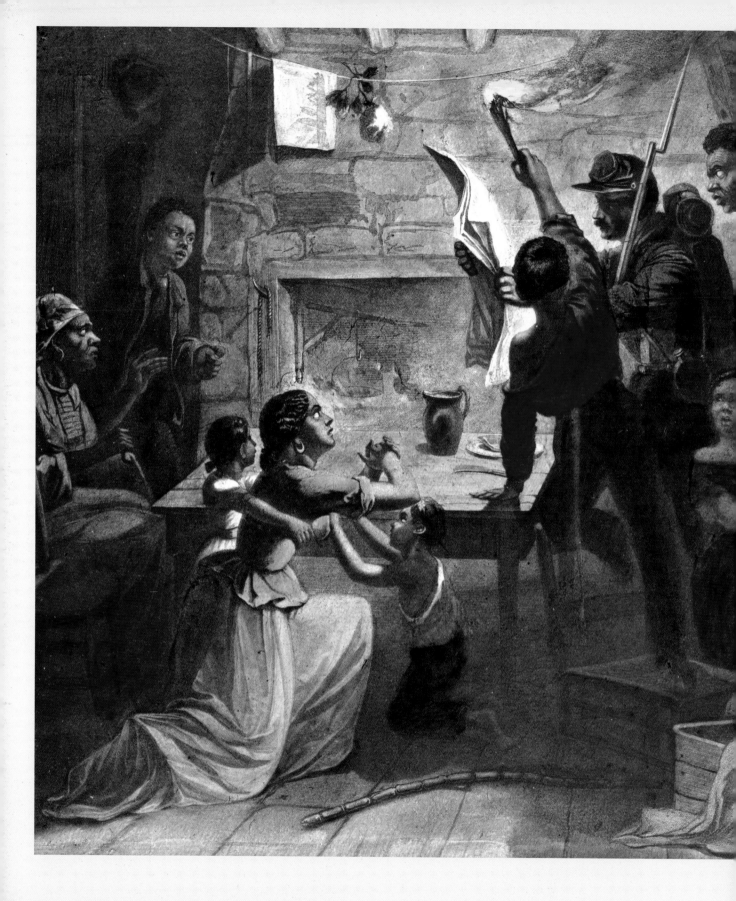

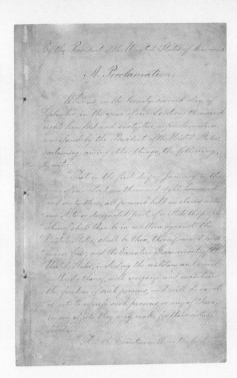

On January 1, 1863, President Abraham Lincoln issued the Emancipation Proclamation, which declared that "all persons held as slaves within any State . . . in rebellion against the United States, shall be then, thenceforward, and forever free" (see fig.).

Lincoln's executive order was limited. As a strategic war measure designed to cripple the Confederacy, it applied only to Confederate territories—which federal forces did not control—while leaving slavery intact in slaveholding states loyal to the Union. Nevertheless, the Emancipation Proclamation marked a historic realignment of the war's objective from preserving the Union to abolishing slavery.

For Black Americans, the Emancipation Proclamation confirmed their convictions that the Civil War was a war for freedom. This order also authorized the enlistment of Black men in the military, spurring the development of the U.S. Colored Troops (USCT).

[left] *Emancipation Proclamation First Read to Negro Slaves*, collodion transparency with applied color, from the *Life of Lincoln: Additional View* series (Philadelphia: C. W. Briggs Company, 1881–1909).
George Eastman Museum/Getty Images

[above] First page of President Abraham Lincoln's Emancipation Proclamation, January 1, 1863.
Presidential Proclamations, 1791–1991, Record Group 11, General Records of the United States Government, National Archives

3
PROGRESS AND BACKLASH, 1865–1950

CHAPTER 3: PROGRESS AND BACKLASH, 1865–1950

At the end of the Civil War, Virginia and other Southern states had to reconfigure their political, economic, and social systems after slavery. Eager to determine their own destinies, formerly enslaved men and women (freedpeople) embraced the new rights and opportunities promised by emancipation. Yet, freedom did not translate into equality, as many white Americans rejected Black people as their equals. This chapter explores the advances and setbacks Black Americans experienced in their struggle for freedom from 1865 through 1950—a period that witnessed remarkable progress but also backlash in the form of disenfranchisement, segregation, and white supremacist violence.

Reconstruction and Re-entrenchment

Reconstruction (1865–1877) was a tumultuous time, as the nation reunited after a bitterly fought war. Initially, President Andrew Johnson managed the terms by which Confederate states would regain their congressional seats. His leniency toward the rebels and hostility to Black equality led to many former Confederates retaining political power. Southern states enacted laws known as Black Codes to reassert control over freedpeople. Virginia's Vagrancy Act of 1866, for example, targeted Black individuals displaced by the war and seeking work. This act reproduced slavery by permitting municipalities to forcibly employ anyone deemed jobless or homeless. It also set precedents for the mass incarceration of Black people and the use of convict labor.

Johnson's actions—especially his pardoning of former Confederates—enraged congressional Republicans. Congress took over Reconstruction and passed key legislation. The Civil Rights Act of 1866 conferred citizenship and equal rights on anyone born in the United States, including the formerly enslaved but excepting Native

Americans—although the act lacked enforcement powers. The 1867 Reconstruction Act put Southern states under U.S. military supervision and required them to "reconstruct" their constitutions, grant certain rights to Black people, and ratify the Fourteenth Amendment (see "Reconstruction Amendments," p. 100).

In 1869, Virginia ratified a new constitution reflecting the priorities of reform-minded Republicans, who led the statewide convention for rewriting this document. Black men also played a role: they helped elect delegates in October 1867—the first time in Virginia's history that Black people voted—and they held twenty-four (all Republican) of 105 delegate positions. This new constitution granted universal male suffrage and established a statewide public school system. The U.S. military withdrew from Virginia in 1870.

For the next few decades, Black men voted in large numbers and served in local and state office (see entry on Peter Jacob Carter, p. 104). However, these political gains were short-lived. Virginia's conservative Democratic Party—which was opposed to Black equality and made up of prewar elites and former Confederates—regained a majority in the state government and worked to disenfranchise Black men through redistricting, voter restrictions, and intimidation. As Reconstruction ended nationally in 1877 and the federal government retreated from protecting Black rights, white control again became entrenched throughout the South.

Virginia's 1902 state constitution marked the culmination of efforts to suppress the Black vote. This new constitution instituted several provisions designed "with a view to the elimination of every negro voter who can be gotten rid of."[66] The most effective provision was a poll tax of $1.50 (about $40 today), which had to be paid for each of the preceding three years. Many Virginians, regardless of their race, could not afford this tax, although Confederate veterans and their sons were exempt. Another measure gave county registrars broad discretion in administering an understanding clause to determine who could vote, based on his ability to read and explain any part of the state constitution.

By 1904, the number of Black voters had dropped by 90 percent, and the number of white voters by 50 percent.[67] Disenfranchisement measures similarly impacted Black and low-income women after the Nineteenth Amendment granted female suffrage (1920). In addition, Virginia's Republican Party largely abandoned supporting Black candidates and constituents in order to attract white voters. Black political participation remained low, and the Democratic Party maintained its grip on state politics until the 1960s.

Forging New Lives

In the wake of emancipation, formerly enslaved individuals faced the challenges of finding family members separated by slavery, securing jobs and housing, and establishing communities. For several years following its 1865 creation, the U.S. Bureau of Refugees, Freedmen, and

"The State Convention at Richmond, Va., in Session," illustration of the constitutional convention, which included black delegates, from *Frank Leslie's Illustrated Newspaper*, February 15, 1868.
Library of Virginia

Abandoned Lands—known as the Freedmen's Bureau—provided schooling, legal assistance in negotiating labor contracts, and other services; charitable organizations, including Black-run ones, also helped in these efforts.

With the transition to a free-labor economy, many Black Virginians continued working in agriculture, but now as wage laborers or sharecroppers. Under sharecropping, a tenant farmed a plot of land in exchange for a portion of the harvest—an arrangement that often favored landowners and kept the tenant in cycles of debt. Black families also acquired land, although their farms were usually small. Farming was a hardscrabble life, but it offered landowners a degree of autonomy, security, and status.[68]

Others escaped the fields, relocating to towns and cities for better-paying jobs in the factories, ports, mines, and other industries that drove

The Thirteenth, Fourteenth, and Fifteenth Amendments to the U.S. Constitution fundamentally altered the nature of American democracy. They abolished slavery forever and guaranteed certain rights—not just for Black people but for all Americans. These Amendments represented the most significant reconceptualization of Americans' rights since the Bill of Rights (1791).

1865

THIRTEENTH AMENDMENT

ENDS SLAVERY IN THE UNITED STATES

"Neither slavery nor involuntary servitude . . . shall exist within the United States, or any place subject to their jurisdiction."

1868

FOURTEENTH AMENDMENT

DEFINES CITIZENS AS ALL INDIVIDUALS BORN OR NATURALIZED IN THE UNITED STATES AND GRANTS CITIZENSHIP TO FORMERLY ENSLAVED PEOPLE

REQUIRES DUE PROCESS AND EQUAL PROTECTION UNDER THE LAW

"Nor shall any State deprive any person of life, liberty, or property, without due process of law; nor deny to any person within its jurisdiction the equal protection of the laws."

1870

FIFTEENTH AMENDMENT

GUARANTEES VOTING RIGHTS OF BLACK MEN

"The right of citizens of the United States to vote shall not be denied or abridged by the United States or by any State on account of race, color, or previous condition of servitude."

[right] Alfred Waud, "The First Vote," illustration from *Harper's Weekly*, November 16, 1867.
Library of Congress

HARPER'S WEEKLY.

A JOURNAL OF CIVILIZATION.

VOL. XI.—No. 568.]   NEW YORK, SATURDAY, NOVEMBER 16, 1867.   [SINGLE COPIES TEN CENTS. $4.00 PER YEAR IN ADVANCE.

Entered according to Act of Congress, in the Year 1867, by Harper & Brothers, in the Clerk's Office of the District Court for the Southern District of New York.

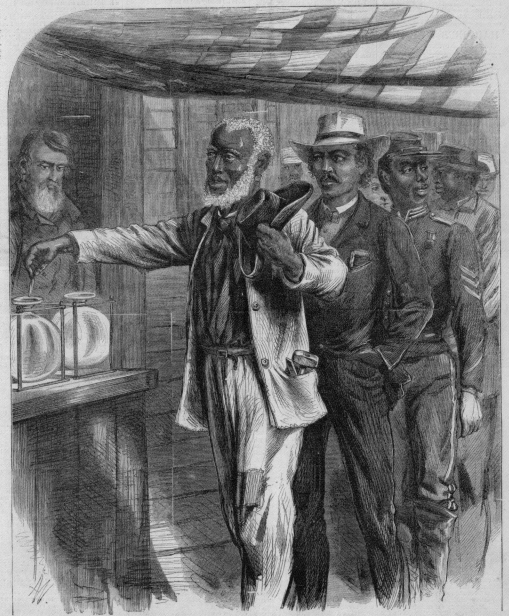

"THE FIRST VOTE."—Drawn by A. R. Waud.—[See next Page.]

DEVOTED TEACHER

MARY S. PEAKE (1823–1862)

During slavery, most Black Virginians were illiterate. State laws restricted the teaching of both enslaved and free Black people to read and write. Many white Southerners feared that Black literacy would undermine racist assumptions of Black intellectual inferiority, while also inciting such rebellious actions as forging freedom papers, reading abolitionist texts, and plotting insurrection. Yet, Black Americans hungered for education, and with emancipation they finally got the opportunity. Black literacy exploded from less than 10 percent in the antebellum period to 30 percent after the war, to 70 percent by 1910.[74]

Mary S. Peake was a pioneering educator who risked her life to teach Black people and helped lay the groundwork for post-war Black schools. Born free in Norfolk, she was sent as a young girl to Alexandria—then part of the District of Columbia—to attend school. In 1839, when Congress passed a law prohibiting Black schools in D.C., Peake returned to Virginia, living first in Norfolk and then in Hampton. She started holding clandestine classes in her home to teach enslaved and free Black people of all ages to read and write. She also founded a charitable organization, the Daughters of Zion, to provide aid to the needy.

At the outbreak of the Civil War, Peake and her family became part of the growing community of Black refugees—including thousands of escaped slaves—seeking safety around Fort Monroe, a U.S. Army stronghold (see "Civil War Contrabands," p. 86). She continued teaching, holding classes for "contrabands" under the boughs of a large oak tree. Her efforts garnered the attention of the Rev. Lewis C. Lockwood, a white agent of the American Missionary Association (AMA), who described

Black students with teacher James Heywood Blackwell, late 19th century.
The Valentine

Peake as "a teacher of the choicest spirit and peculiar [extraordinary] qualifications."[75] An abolitionist missionary organization founded in 1846 in New York, the AMA helped establish hundreds of Black schools and colleges throughout the South during Reconstruction.

In September 1861, the AMA hired Peake for its first freedmen's school in Hampton. She conducted lessons in a cottage and, to meet popular demand, added evening classes for adults. In a January 1862 letter to the AMA, Peake reported "53 [students] in the day school and 20 in the night" (see fig.). She continued working despite failing health from tuberculosis. Lockwood described how "her pupils would be found around her [bed], drawing knowledge as it were from her very life"— a testament to her and her students' dedication.[76]

Peake's legacy endured long after her untimely death at age thirty-nine. She proved the desire and capacity for learning among Black people. As one of her students remarked, "We want to get wisdom. That is all we need. Let us get that, and we are made for time and eternity."[77] Her school became a model for other freedmen's schools, and her cottage became part of Hampton Normal and Agricultural Institute (now Hampton University). The oak tree under which Peake taught still stands and is called Emancipation Oak because, in 1863, escaped slaves gathered here to listen to a reading of the Emancipation Proclamation.

[below left] Mary S. Peake, about 1860.
Courtesy of Hampton University Archives

[below right] Letter from Mary S. Peake to Simeon Smith Jocelyn, January 1862.
American Missionary Association Archives, H1-4364, Amistad Research Center, Tulane University

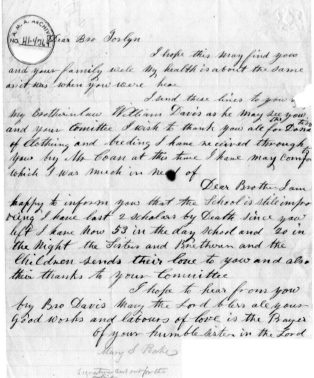

BLACK POLITICAL LEADERSHIP

PETER JACOB CARTER (1845–1886)

As soon as the Civil War ended, Black people began demanding the rights of full citizenship, including having a voice in government. Black men formed political clubs and exercised their newfound right to vote, enshrined in Virginia's reconstructed constitution and the Fifteenth Amendment. (Women, Black and white, did not gain the franchise until the Nineteenth Amendment of 1920.) They also won election to public office, holding a small but influential minority in Virginia's government.[78]

Peter Jacob Carter was among the 100 Black legislators who served in the General Assembly between 1869 and 1900. Born into slavery on the Eastern Shore, he escaped and enlisted in the U.S. Colored Infantry in 1863. After the Civil War, Carter attended Hampton Normal and Agricultural Institute (now Hampton University) and then got involved in politics. He represented Northampton County as a Republican delegate for four terms from 1871 to 1879—becoming one of the leading and longest-serving Black politicians in this era. Known for his oratorical skills, Carter worked on a range of issues, from those affecting his local constituents, such as taxes on oystermen and electoral boundaries, to broader concerns, including Black jury service and banishing the whipping post as a form of punishment. As a sign of his stature, he served as sergeant-at-arms at the Republican State Convention of 1875, as well as on various committees and delegations.

Carter entered Virginia politics at a time of great upheaval—of party realignments and new alliances, as well as deep divides over Black rights and fiscal priorities. During Reconstruction, so-called radical Republicans made up of white Union loyalists and Black men held a majority in the state government. Virginia's new constitution of 1869 reflected Republican priorities of universal male suffrage and the establishment of a free, statewide public school system. (A provision to

Peter J. Carter, photograph from Luther Porter Jackson, *Negro Office-Holders in Virginia* (Norfolk: Guide Quality Press, 1945).
VMHC

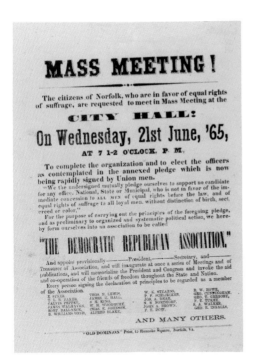

[above left] Notice of
meeting for equal suffrage,
Democratic Republican
Association (Norfolk),
June 21, 1865.
VMHC

[above right] King George
County "colored" ballot
box, 1867.
Courtesy of Library of Virginia

disenfranchise former Confederates failed.) After Reconstruction ended
in Virginia in 1870, the Democratic Party—led by white elites and former
Confederates—began to regain power. Along with conservative white
Republicans who were also opposed to Black equality, the Democrats
started chipping away at Black gains. Peter Carter became one of many
Black politicians who lost his seat to gerrymandering (the manipulation
of voting district boundaries). He joined the Readjuster Party, which
emerged in opposition to Virginia's white elite establishment.[79]

A broad interracial coalition of Black Virginians, white farmers and
working men, and Republicans and Democrats, the Readjuster Party
briefly controlled the state government from 1879 to 1883. Its platform
promoted Black suffrage, as well as readjusting or refinancing the state's
debt in order to preserve funding for public schools and other services.
Democrats mobilized against the biracial Readjusters using racist
fearmongering of "negro dominance" to draw away white support.[80]
By the mid-1880s, the Democratic Party regained control of the state
government and embarked on a successful agenda of maintaining white
supremacy and disenfranchising Black and poor white Virginians. After
a flourishing of Black political participation in the postwar decades, no
Black person held state office between 1895 and 1968.

PROGRESS THROUGH RESPECTABILITY

BOOKER T. WASHINGTON (1856–1915)

As the title of his autobiography declares, Booker T. Washington rose "up from slavery" to national prominence as the foremost Black educator and orator in late 19th- and early 20th-century America. His own remarkable life story exemplified his philosophy of Black progress through educational and economic opportunity—a vision that was highly influential, but one that also put him at odds with other Black leaders calling for political and social equality.

Born enslaved in rural Franklin County, Washington experienced firsthand the jubilation and disorientation of emancipation as newly freed Black Southerners had to navigate the exigencies of procuring wages, housing, and other necessities. As a young freedman, he helped support his family—now living in West Virginia—by working in salt furnaces and coal mines. In 1872, "determined to secure an education," Washington walked and begged wagon rides to cover the long trek to eastern Virginia to attend Hampton Normal and Agricultural Institute (now Hampton University).[81] An excellent student, he graduated at the top of his class and returned to Hampton to teach.

In 1881, the Alabama legislature hired Washington to create a Black vocational school in Tuskegee. He built from the ground up what would become the Tuskegee Institute, transforming an idea into a campus with more than 1,100 students, eighty buildings, and thirty-five majors by 1900. His early experience with poverty drove his commitment to producing financially self-sufficient graduates. To that end, the curriculum focused on practical and industrial trades, such as teaching, carpentry, printing, farming, and sewing.

As the Tuskegee Institute grew more successful, Washington rose in national stature and was in high demand as a public speaker and advisor. Presidents Theodore Roosevelt and William Howard Taft consulted him on race relations and, in 1901, Washington became the first Black

Booker T. Washington, about 1900, photographed by The Scurlock Studio, Washington, D.C.
VMHC

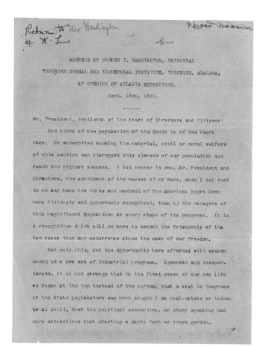

person invited to dine at the White House. He also published books and founded the National Negro Business League (1900).

Washington's doctrine of Black self-reliance, hard work, and respectability won broad acclaim. Many Black Southerners embraced this vision as a route to escaping the debt and dependency of sharecropping. It also appealed to white people because it maintained existing racial hierarchies by promoting manual labor. Washington urged Black Americans to acquiesce to segregation and discrimination, and to focus on gaining economic security first, in preparation for gradual progress toward equality:

> No race can prosper till it learns that there is as much dignity in tilling a field as in writing a poem. It is at the bottom of life we must begin and not the top. Nor should we permit our grievances to overshadow our opportunities.[82]

Washington's accommodationist stance—of working within the existing system—drew criticism from more progressive Black leaders such as W. E. B. Du Bois (1868–1963). A scholar, sociologist, and founder of the National Association for the Advancement of Colored People (NAACP, 1909), Du Bois advocated confrontation and protest to demand civil rights. The different approaches to Black advancement represented by Washington and Du Bois continue to animate debates about how to bring about social change and racial equity today.

[above right] Mechanical drawing class at Tuskegee Institute, about 1902.
Library of Congress

[above left] First page of Booker T. Washington's "Atlanta Exposition Speech," September 18, 1895.
Booker T. Washington Papers, Library of Congress

[left] Gregory H. Swanson at the University of Virginia, September 15, 1950.
University of Virginia Visual History Collection (RG-30/1/10.011, Print 10495). Albert and Shirley Small Special Collections Library, University of Virginia

[below] Virginia Union University students and faculty, 1912–1913.
Virginia Union University, Archives and Special Collections

Virginia established its first Black colleges after the Civil War. These new institutions fueled Black educational achievements, as well as professional opportunities and networks. The state's historically Black colleges and universities (HBCUs)—by their present-day names—include Virginia Union University (Richmond, 1865), Hampton University (1868), Virginia State University (Petersburg, 1882), Virginia University of Lynchburg (1886), and Norfolk State University (1935).

Yet Black Virginians could not earn graduate and professional degrees, which were only offered at the state's "white" universities. Prompted by Alice Jackson Stuart's rejection from a graduate program at the University of Virginia (UVA) in 1935, civil rights activists began pressuring the General Assembly to offer such opportunities. Rather than desegregating the state's universities, the Commonwealth established a graduate program at Virginia State University, a Black school, and paid for Black students to attend out-of-state schools. In 1950, when Gregory Swanson registered at UVA's School of Law, he became the first Black person admitted to a historically all-white public university in Virginia.

"THE FIGHTING EDITOR"

JOHN MITCHELL, JR. (1863–1929)

"He is a man who would walk into the jaws of death to serve his race."[83]

One of the most important civic figures in Progressive-era Richmond, John Mitchell, Jr., fought tirelessly to advance Black communities in the face of systemic racism. He made his deepest impact as the editor and publisher of the *Richmond Planet* for more than forty years. Born into slavery and educated in freedmen's schools, Mitchell took the helm of this fledgling weekly paper in 1884 at age twenty-one and transformed it into one of the largest circulating Black newspapers in the South. He used this platform—and his pen—to champion civil rights, racial justice, and Black pride amid the codification of Jim Crow segregation and an upsurge of white supremacist violence. "Stand up like men!" he urged his readers, "Don't cringe and cower. Demand your rights with manly dignity."[84]

Mitchell earned the nickname "The Fighting Editor" for his fiery rhetoric, unflinching coverage of racial issues, and willingness to court controversy. He first gained fame for his reporting on lynching and, with his friend and fellow journalist Ida B. Wells, he helped launch a national antilynching campaign. In addition to documenting these atrocities—in the 1890s, a lynching death occurred every two days on average—Mitchell encouraged Black resistance. "The best remedy for a lyncher or a cursed midnight rider," he wrote, "is a 16-shot Winchester

rifle in the hands of a dead-shot Negro."[85] This confrontational style made Mitchell the target of white supremacist threats, which he met with his typical daring. For example, upon receiving an anonymous letter from Charlotte County, he traveled to the area with pistols strapped to his hip. "The cowardly letter writer was nowhere in evidence," he reported.[86]

In the pages of the *Planet*, Mitchell also lobbied for equitable services for Black communities, the just treatment of Black prisoners, and other civil rights causes. For instance, when Richmond streetcars started segregating passengers by race in 1904, he and his friend Maggie Lena Walker started a boycott that lasted two years. In a pointed reference to the hypocrisy of segregation in public spaces, he wrote: "White men who mixed the races and gave us our crop of white Negroes didn't do it on the street cars."[87] As a sign of his national influence, he served as president of the Afro-American Press Association from 1890 to 1894.

The indefatigable Mitchell was also actively engaged in the political, religious, and business life of Richmond's Jackson Ward neighborhood. Dubbed "America's Black Wall Street" and the "Harlem of the South," this district was a thriving hub of Black entrepreneurship and culture. Among his many civic activities, Mitchell represented Jackson Ward on the city council from 1888 to 1896; chartered the Mechanics Savings Bank in 1901; and led the Colored Knights of Pythias, a benevolent fraternal organization that provided camaraderie as well as insurance and other benefits to its members. Mitchell recognized that Black communities had to help themselves to combat the increasingly oppressive effects of Jim Crow.

Front page of the *Richmond Planet*, with an article about the lynching of John Henry James of Charlottesville, July 16, 1898.

Chronicling America: Historic American Newspapers. Library of Congress

COLORED
SEATED IN REAR

B & B SIGN CO.   AUGUST 1, 1929

[above] A segregated bus, photographed by Stan Wayman, from *Life*, May 7, 1956.

[left] "Colored" sign for segregated seating, printed by B. & B. Sign Company, 1929.
VMHC

In the late 19th century, white Southerners reasserted their sense of superiority over Black people by adopting segregation. Homer Plessy, a mixed-race man, challenged a Louisiana law requiring separate railway cars for Black and white passengers. In 1896, the U.S. Supreme Court ruled that "separate but equal" facilities *were* constitutional.[88] This landmark decision provided the legal basis for racial segregation in public transportation, restaurants, parks, theaters, and other facilities across the South.

In the wake of *Plessy* v. *Ferguson*, Virginia and other states passed statutes mandating segregation. Separate "colored only" amenities, however, were rarely equal to those for "whites only." This legalized racial caste system, known as Jim Crow, lasted until the 1960s and treated Black people like second-class citizens— relegated to the back of the bus. Black communities fought back by developing a parallel economy of establishments to serve people of color.

NEW NEGRO POET

ANNE SPENCER (1882–1975)

A renowned poet and civil rights activist, Anne Spencer was part of the flourishing of Black culture in the 1920s known as the New Negro Movement or Harlem Renaissance. Stimulated in part by the migration of Black people to urban centers and by an ethos of change after World War I, African American intellectuals, writers, artists, dancers, and musicians produced a distinctive and diverse array of works that celebrated Black self-determination and artistic expression as means of social and political transformation. New York City's Harlem neighborhood was the movement's epicenter, with other important hubs including Detroit, Chicago, and Los Angeles—and Spencer's home in Lynchburg, Virginia.

Anne Spencer was born Annie Bethel Bannister in rural Henry County. She attended Virginia Seminary (now Virginia University of Lynchburg), a Black boarding school where she fell in love with literature and her future husband, Edward Spencer. In 1901, the Spencers settled in Lynchburg, where they built a house with extensive gardens.

In 1917, Anne Spencer met the writer and activist James Weldon Johnson when he came to Lynchburg to help her establish a chapter of the National Association for the Advancement of Colored People (NAACP)—one of the first in Virginia. Johnson encouraged her writing and brought her into the orbit of the New Negro Movement. She befriended many leading Black writers with whom she regularly shared works and critiques. A self-described "scribbler," Spencer was always "jotting things down here, there and everywhere"—on receipts, used envelopes, and scraps of paper—yet she was reluctant to publish

Dolly Allen Mason, *The Cocktail Party*, about 1940, mural painting from the Spencer House.
Anne Spencer House and Garden Museum, Inc. Archives

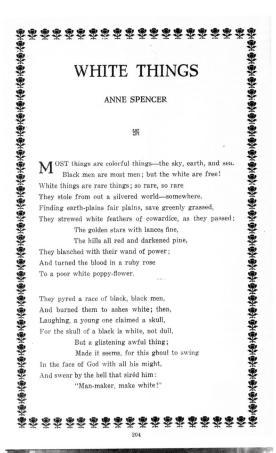

WHITE THINGS

ANNE SPENCER

卐

MOST things are colorful things—the sky, earth, and sea.
    Black men are most men; but the white are free!
White things are rare things; so rare, so rare
They stole from out a silvered world—somewhere.
Finding earth-plains fair plains, save greenly grassed,
They strewed white feathers of cowardice, as they passed;
        The golden stars with lances fine,
        The hills all red and darkened pine,
They blanched with their wand of power;
And turned the blood in a ruby rose
To a poor white poppy-flower.

They pyred a race of black, black men,
And burned them to ashes white; then,
Laughing, a young one claimed a skull,
For the skull of a black is white, not dull,
        But a glistening awful thing;
        Made it seems, for this ghoul to swing
In the face of God with all his might,
And swear by the hell that siréd him:
        "Man-maker, make white!"

204

despite frequent requests.[89] During the 1920s and '30s, only about thirty of her poems appeared in literary magazines and anthologies.

Critics praised her lyrical style and original voice. Many of her poems thematize renewal, the interconnectedness of humans and nature, and the spiritual continuity of life and death. For example, "Change" (1931) begins:

This day is here I hoped would come at last,
When I, a man, should live again a tree
The dregs I drained with Life in days long passed
Now thru my body course in ecstasy.[90]

Spencer also addressed racial problems, as in "White Things" (1923), which evokes racism and lynching while asserting the common humanity among the races—"For the skull of a black is white" (see fig.). She was the second Black writer featured in the *Norton Anthology of Modern Poetry* (1973).

Spencer's home became a famous gathering place and salon for Black luminaries. Sterling A. Brown, Countee Cullen, W. E. B. Du Bois, Langston Hughes, Zora Neale Hurston, Claude McKay, and Paul Robeson were among her regular guests. These friends valued the lively intellectual exchange she fostered.

Throughout her life, Spencer remained committed to civil rights activism and to following her own path—often challenging racial and social conventions. For instance, she refused to ride segregated buses and she scandalized townspeople by wearing trousers in public. While working as the librarian of Lynchburg's segregated high school from 1923 to 1945, Spencer fought for resources for Black students. As she wrote in an unpublished poem, "Being a Negro Woman is the world's most exciting game of 'Taboo.'"[91]

[above] Anne Spencer, "White Things," from *The Crisis* 25 (March 1923): 204.
Internet Archive, University of Illinois Urbana-Champaign

[left] Anne Spencer, early 20th century.
Anne Spencer House and Garden Museum, Inc. Archives

EUGENICS AND MARRIAGE LAW

RICHARD (1933–1975) AND MILDRED LOVING (1939–2008)

Richard and Mildred Loving were appellants in the U.S. Supreme Court decision that declared bans on interracial marriage unconstitutional.[92] One of the landmark civil rights victories of the 1960s, their case was rooted in racist policies of the 1920s. This earlier decade witnessed the heyday of the eugenics movement. The now-discredited field of eugenics claimed that the white race was genetically superior to other races and that racial mixing would have a ruinous effect on society. This pseudo-science provided justification for white supremacy and anti-immigration xenophobia in America, as well as for the genocide of European Jews in Nazi Germany.

Virginia was a hotbed of eugenics, with influential figures of the movement in the state government and universities.[93] They successfully lobbied the General Assembly to pass a series of Racial Integrity Acts from 1924 to 1930 to protect the "purity" of the white race. These laws strengthened the ban on interracial marriage with stricter classifications of racial identity. A "colored" person was anyone with even one drop of non-white blood. Such attempts to define racial categories denied the historical realities that European, African, and Native peoples had been mixing for centuries, and that many Virginians had mixed ancestry resulting from the sexual exploitation of enslaved women.

For Richard Loving and Mildred Jeter of rural Caroline County, their love saw no color line. Because he was white and she identified as Black and American Indian, they had to travel to Washington, D.C., to marry in June 1958. The following month, the county sheriff arrested them in a nighttime raid for violating the interracial marriage ban of the Racial Integrity Acts—a felony offense.

The Lovings initially agreed to leave Virginia for twenty-five years to avoid a jail sentence, then decided to fight back because they missed their home and family. In 1963, Mildred sought help from the U.S.

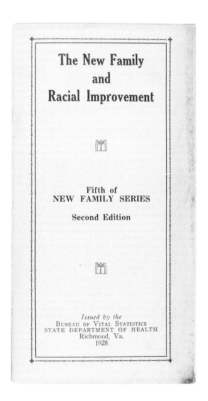

The New Family
and
Racial Improvement

Fifth of
NEW FAMILY SERIES

Second Edition

Issued by the
BUREAU OF VITAL STATISTICS
STATE DEPARTMENT OF HEALTH
Richmond, Va.
1928

Dr. Walter Plecker, *The New Family and Racial Improvement*, pamphlet espousing white supremacy and eugenics (Richmond: Bureau of Vital Statistics, 1925). VMHC

1151 Neal St.
N.E. Wash. D.C.
June 20, 1963

Dear sir:

I am writing to you concerning a problem we have.

5 yrs. ago my husband and I were married here in the District. We then returned to Va. to live. My husband is White, I am part negro, & part indian.

At the time we did not know there was a law in Va. against mixed marriages.

Therefore we were jailed and tried in a little town of Bowling Green.

We were to leave the state to make our home.

The problem is we are not allowed to visit our families. The judge said if we enter the state within the next 30 yrs, that we will have to spend 1 yr. in jail.

We know we can't live there, but we would like to go back once and awhile to visit our families & friends.

We have 3 children and cannot afford an attorney.

We wrote to the Attorney General, he suggested that we get in touch with you.

[above left] Mildred and Richard Loving after the Supreme Court decision, June 12, 1967.
Associated Press

[above right] Letter from Mildred Loving to the U.S. Attorney General, June 20, 1963.
Courtesy of Philip Hirschkop, ACLU counsel to the Lovings

Attorney General, Robert Kennedy, who forwarded her letter to the American Civil Liberties Union (ACLU; see fig.). The ACLU took on their case, which ultimately landed at the U.S. Supreme Court. Richard instructed his lawyers, "Tell the Court that I love my wife, and it is just unfair that I can't live with her in Virginia."[94]

In the 1967 decision *Loving* v. *Virginia*, the Supreme Court struck down Virginia's prohibition of interracial marriage—and similar bans in other states—as a violation of the Fourteenth Amendment's guarantee of due process and equal protection under the law, declaring:

> Marriage is one of the "basic civil rights of man," fundamental to our very existence and survival. . . . [T]he freedom to marry, or not marry, a person of another race resides with the individual, and cannot be infringed by the State.[95]

The Lovings returned to Virginia and to a quiet life, but their case had a far-reaching impact. In 2015, the Supreme Court cited *Loving* v. *Virginia* as a precedent for *Obergefell* v. *Hodges*, which legalized same-sex marriage—an example of how the fight for Black equality has also advanced the civil rights of other groups.

SEEKING A BETTER LIFE AND THE GREAT MIGRATION

MARY JOHNSON SPROW (1885–1981)

During the first half of the 20th century, many Black Southerners sought better lives by moving away, becoming part of a mass exodus known as the Great Migration. They left for better employment and educational opportunities, as well as to escape the suffocating oppression of segregation, disenfranchisement, and violent intimidation in the Jim Crow South. Between 1900 and 1950, about four million people—nearly half of Black America—relocated from rural areas in the South to industrial cities in the North and West, such as New York, Pittsburgh, Chicago, Detroit, and Los Angeles. Virginia lost half of its Black residents.[96] The Great Migration transformed America's Black population from a largely rural to a predominantly urban one and reshaped the nation's social, political, and cultural identity.

Mary Johnson Sprow was one of the many Black Virginians who pursued the promise of greater economic security and personal freedom in the city. Part of a large family from rural Culpeper County, she received a few years of schooling—"just about enough so you don't have to make an X [to sign your name]"—before she had to start earning for the household.[97] At age twelve, Sprow left the family farm and moved to Washington, D.C. In a typical pattern of chain migration, several of her siblings were already established in the city. They helped her secure work and provided a support network; all of them also sent money home to Virginia.

For a poor Black girl from rural Virginia, job prospects were generally limited to household service. In 1910, 90 percent of Black female laborers in Washington worked as servants—as did Mary Sprow for more than sixty years.[98] Despite such limitations, she found autonomy and fulfillment living in the city. The diary Sprow kept from 1916 to 1918 documents her efforts to establish her independence. One of her primary goals during these years was to switch from live-in service,

Mary Johnson (later Sprow), about 1910.

Courtesy of Abena Lewis-Mhoon Collection

FAMILY RECORD.

The Children of Marlton and Rina Dickson Dickson
BIRTHS.

Eliza, born Dec 6th 1852

Douglas, born Jan 14th 1855

Caroline, born April 6th 1857

Indy, born Jan 18th 1859

Alice, born August 2nd 1861

Jeff, born March 7th 1864

Lewis Long, born July 17th 1866

Anna born Jan 21st 1869

Emma born Aug 1st 1871

Alice died Nov 1st 1960

Eliza and Peyton Johnson

Charles E. Born Feb 20 187_ — Died July 4 1953

Fred L. Born Oct 28th 1878 — Died 3-24-194_

Senator B. Born Jan 21th 18__ — died 1880 And died May 12th 1880

Memphis B. Born May 12th 1__

Hunter F. Born Aug. 4th 188_ — Died Dec 31 1937

Rina Born Feb 15th 1884, and — Died 1883 died Sept 10th 1884

Mary E. and Walter H. born — Died July 20 195_ March 30th 1885

Amy B. Born Aug 16th 1__

Gertrude born Jan 16 188_ — Died 1943 Dec 2

Marion V born Mon. May 2_ 18_

Brown Nector Julie 1st 1890

Lillian Born January 13 189_ — Died Dec 1947 (words)

Julia A Born July 31th 1893

Kate Born march 30 friday 18_
18_

Pages from the Johnson family Bible (1875) showing the record of family births and deaths; Mary Johnson Sprow appears halfway down the right-hand page.

Courtesy of Abena Lewis-Mhoon Collection

in which she resided in her white employer's home and was on call virtually 24/7, to day work or "living out," which offered greater control of her own life. Vowing "I will, I will, I will," she made the transition in 1916 against her family's wishes. "Sister is still cross that I am not living-in," Sprow reported. "I can do for me."[99]

In Washington, she enjoyed an active social life, going to dances, movies, and parties, and dating suitors. Working-class Black women like Sprow also supported each other through saving clubs, insurance groups, and other mutual aid organizations. Always strong-willed, she defied her family again in her choice of a husband, Luray Sprow, a gardener. Mary Sprow also engaged in minor acts of rebellion at work: she dusted very slowly so that she could read her employer's books while working.[100]

Sprow exemplifies the determination and experience of many Black people who made the Great Migration from South to North, from rural to urban areas. Although she still faced hardships and racism, she found a vibrant community and improved opportunities in her new home.

TICKETS

12

Jacob Lawrence, *The railroad stations were at times so over-packed with people that special guards had to be called in to keep order*, casein tempera on hardboard, from *The Migration Series*, 1940–1941.

BREAKING BARRIERS IN WARTIME

CLEMENCEAU GIVINGS (1919–1944)

"This able and courageous officer . . . made the supreme sacrifice to preserve the ideals of freedom and justice that we cherish."
– General H. H. Arnold, Commander, Army Air Forces, 1944[101]

When World War II broke out in 1939, the U.S. armed forces—like the federal government and much of American society—were racially segregated. Black service members faced pervasive discrimination and prejudice. Many military leaders embraced a deeply racist Army War College report of 1925 characterizing Black soldiers as "mentally inferior to the white man," "by nature subservient," cowardly, and unfit as officers.[102] Black men and women were generally relegated to menial jobs and supporting roles and were denied leadership positions and other opportunities, such as flying combat planes.

As America prepared to enter the war, Black civil rights organizations lobbied for change. Yielding to this pressure, President Franklin D. Roosevelt directed the U.S. Army Air Corps—predecessor of the Air Force—to establish a program in Tuskegee, Alabama, to train Black aviators for military combat. Between 1941 and 1946, nearly 1,000 pilots graduated from this program. An additional 14,600 men and women trained as navigators, bombardiers, mechanics, radio operators, and other service personnel.

In 1943, Clemenceau "Clem" Givings earned his wings as a Tuskegee Airman, the popular name for these pioneering pilots. A native of Richmond and graduate of Virginia Union University, he enlisted in 1941 and entered the Tuskegee Army Flying School the following year. Fascinated with flying since childhood, he wrote to his parents of his passion:

[above] 2nd Lieutenant Clemenceau Givings's "Spit Fire" patch with the insignia of the 332nd Fighter Group (Tuskegee Airmen), about 1944.
VMHC, Gift of Dr. Francis M. Foster, Sr.

[right] 2nd Lieutenant Clemenceau Givings with his plane, about 1944.
VMHC, Gift of Dr. Francis M. Foster, Sr.

Tuskegee Airmen leather flight helmet and goggles belonging to Lt. Earle R. Lane of Ohio, 1944–1945.
Kenneth W. Rendell

I just can't begin to describe the beauty of the sky and sea. . . . It's just another of those things that stresses the magnificence of God and the smallness of mankind in the universe. It compares only with the sensation I feel while flying at high altitude.[103]

He was also a natural fit for the job. A fellow officer described 2nd Lieutenant Givings as "strictly air corps, incorporating in his decorum all the zest, cocksureness, pride and braggadocio that is the essence of a fighter pilot's makeup." Even his speech sounded like "a burst of flak" from antiaircraft fire.[104]

Givings was stationed in Italy in January 1944 as part of the 100th Squadron, 332nd Fighter Group. He saw action in the months-long Allied offensive against German forces in Anzio, south of Rome. On March 18, 1944, Givings died when his plane crashed due to engine failure during a coastal patrol. He was only twenty-four years old and one of eighty-four Tuskegee Airmen to make the ultimate sacrifice.

As the first Black pilots in the U.S. armed forces, the Tuskegee Airmen had an immediate and lasting impact. Through their phenomenal success in the war, they refuted racist doubts about their abilities and opened doors for Black men and women in other branches of the military. The heroism of the Tuskegee Airmen and other Black service members also influenced President Truman's milestone decision to desegregate the armed services in 1948.[105]

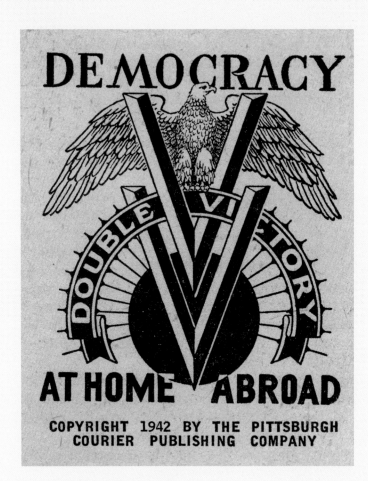

COPYRIGHT 1942 BY THE PITTSBURGH COURIER PUBLISHING COMPANY

*". . . you say we're fighting
For democracy.
Then why don't democracy
Include me?*

*I ask you this question
Cause I want to know
How long I got to fight
BOTH HITLER —
AND JIM CROW."*

– Langston Hughes, from
"Beaumont to Detroit: 1943"[106]

Double V campaign
logo, from the *Pittsburgh
Courier*, 1942.
Newseum Collection

Black men and women have served on the front lines and in supporting roles in every American war—from the Revolution to current conflicts around the globe. Yet, historically, their service and sacrifices were not rewarded with equal treatment. The U.S. military was segregated and Black servicemembers faced discrimination and limited opportunities.

World War II crystallized this contradiction for Black people. Their country asked them to fight totalitarian regimes abroad, while facing oppression in Jim Crow America. Fed up with this injustice, many Black Americans embraced an early civil rights effort called the Double Victory or Double V campaign: a campaign to fight for democracy overseas *and* for full rights of citizenship at home.

Their activism prompted the U.S. government to desegregate the defense industry in 1941 and the armed forces in 1948—both of which had, and continue to have, large presences in Virginia.

Negroes Are
Americans Too
Protect Them
We Demand
THE RIGHT
TO VOTE
EVERY-
WHERE
STOP

4

EQUALITY
ACHIEVED?
1950–2020

CHAPTER 4: EQUALITY ACHIEVED? 1950–2020

Black Americans ushered in the modern era with a determined fight for civil rights that culminated in sweeping changes in the nation's laws and conception of equality. In subsequent decades, Black people broke down barriers in and shaped the contours of all arenas of U.S. society—even the presidency. Yet, despite significant progress toward the ideal of equality, racial disparities persist. America still struggles to overcome deeply embedded patterns of discrimination that took root in 1619.

The Civil Rights Movement

Building on earlier generations of activism, the civil rights movement of the 1950s and '60s mobilized millions of Americans who were fed up with the injustice and indignities of Jim Crow. Black men and women and their allies took the fight for equality to the courts, where they brought lawsuits challenging segregation and discrimination, and to the streets, where they staged mass protests, boycotts, and voter mobilization drives to influence public opinion and lawmakers. Black demands for equality challenged white supremacy, while also highlighting the contradiction between the nation's egalitarian principles and its systemic racism.

Multiple organizations with diverse strategies and tactics joined the freedom struggle. These ranged from the nonviolent civil disobedience and vision of interracial brotherhood advocated by Dr. Martin Luther King, Jr., and his Southern Christian Leadership Conference (SCLC), to the grassroots, non-hierarchical approach of Ella Baker and the Student Nonviolent Coordinating Committee (SNCC), to the militant Black nationalist stance of Malcolm X and the Nation of Islam. The movement also resonated globally with the anticolonization struggles in Africa and with the Cold War's competing claims about the superiority of American democracy or Soviet communism.

Lunch counter stool, about 1950, from the Woolworth Department Store in Richmond, where civil rights activists staged sit-ins in February 1960.
The Valentine

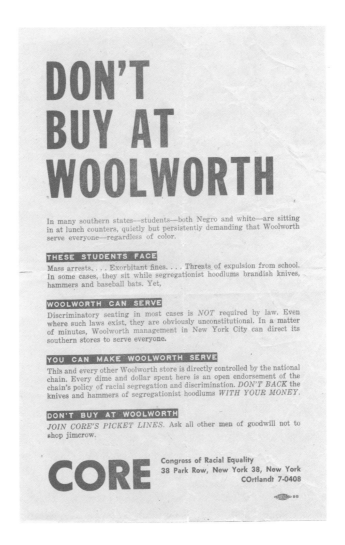

"Don't Buy at Woolworth,"
broadside by the Congress of
Racial Equality (CORE), 1962.
VMHC

Virginians played an important role in the movement, particularly on both sides of the battle over school desegregation (see entry on Barbara Johns Powell and "'From *Brown* to *Green*': Desegregating Schools," pp. 134, 139). Civil rights activists also held protests across Virginia. For instance, Black Richmonders conducted sit-ins and boycotts in 1960 to protest segregation in the city's restaurants and shops. In Danville in 1963, peaceful demonstrations demanding municipal jobs and equal rights for Black citizens met with a police crackdown.[107]

The Black freedom struggle exposed the depth of racial inequality and animosity in America. Despite largely peaceful methods, civil rights activists regularly faced arrest, white mob violence, police beatings, and even death.[108] Their courage, determination, and sacrifice convinced many white Americans of the merits of the cause. In response to pressure from Black leaders, the federal government became more involved in protecting the rights and safety of Black citizens and enforcing the compliance of Southern states with the law.

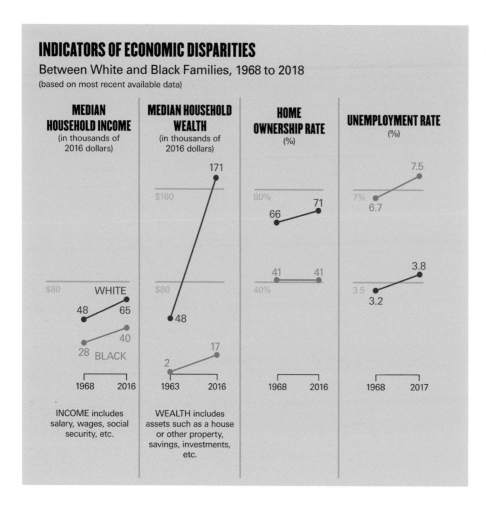

INDICATORS OF ECONOMIC DISPARITIES
Between White and Black Families, 1968 to 2018
(based on most recent available data)

MEDIAN HOUSEHOLD INCOME
(in thousands of 2016 dollars)

WHITE
48 — 65
28 — 40
BLACK

1968 — 2016

INCOME includes salary, wages, social security, etc.

MEDIAN HOUSEHOLD WEALTH
(in thousands of 2016 dollars)

171
$160
$80
48
2 — 17

1963 — 2016

WEALTH includes assets such as a house or other property, savings, investments, etc.

HOME OWNERSHIP RATE
(%)

80%
66 — 71
41 — 41
40%

1968 — 2016

UNEMPLOYMENT RATE
(%)

7.5
7%
6.7
3.5 — 3.8
3.2
40%

1968 — 2017

Adapted from Fred Harris and Alan Curtis, "The Unmet Promise of Equality," *New York Times*, February 28, 2018.

Among the movement's most significant victories was the civil rights legislation passed by Congress the 1960s. These laws banned discrimination in public accommodations, employment, and housing on the basis of race—as well as sex, religion, and national origin—and guaranteed voting rights (see "Landmark Legislation," p. 142).[109] Nearly 200 years after the Declaration of Independence proclaimed that "all men are created equal," this principle was codified into law for *all* Americans.

"From Protest to Politics": The Continuing Fight[110]

The civil rights movement also worked to combat socioeconomic inequalities and build Black political influence. In 1968, many Black Americans still lived in poverty—about 35 percent compared to 10 percent of white people—and lacked access to good housing, schools, and jobs.[111] Deindustrialization and the disinvestment in Black urban neighborhoods that accompanied "white flight" to the suburbs exacerbated these problems (see "Living Disparities," p. 158). Black activists and communities were also regularly subjected to police brutality. Such incidents along with the 1968 assassination of Dr. Martin

Luther King, Jr., sparked uprisings in cities across the nation that, in turn, led to increased policing and the demonization of Black activists.

Black Power emerged in this period as an ideology encompassing a range of ideas, including Black cultural pride, self-determination, self-defense, and Black nationalism. Black Power was manifest in the proliferation of Black political and community organizations, in the establishment of African American Studies programs in universities, and in the more militant stance of such activist groups as the Black Panther Party, founded in 1966.[112]

The Voting Rights Act (1965) and voter mobilization drives led to increased Black political participation. Black Americans voted in unprecedented numbers and won elected office at municipal, state, and federal levels—often for the first time since Reconstruction in Southern states (see entry on L. Douglas Wilder, p. 149). Twenty-two Black Americans served in the U.S. Congress between 1965 and 1980, compared to only seven from 1900 to 1964.[113] The Congressional Black Caucus, formed in 1971, wields its bloc influence on a range of issues.

In the last quarter of the 20th century, Republican politicians embraced the "Southern strategy" to win the support of white voters disaffected by Black gains. This strategy used coded, rather than explicit, references to race, such as "states' rights" to signal resistance to federal enforcement of Black civil rights and "law and order" to demonize civil rights activists.[114] Other targets of white grievance were mandated busing, affirmative action, and "welfare queens."[115]

Another form of backlash to Black progress was the War on Drugs of the 1980s and '90s. "Tough on crime" lawmakers in both political parties passed new and harsher sentencing laws that led to an explosion of America's prison population and the mass incarceration of people of color. Black men are 5.8 times more likely to be incarcerated, and they face longer sentences than white men for the same offenses. The racial bias of America's criminal justice system has had a devastating impact on many communities of color, from over-policing and fatal police encounters to the limitations someone with a criminal record faces in voting, gaining employment, and receiving social services.[116]

Racial In/Equalities in the New Millennium

In recent years, the quest for Black equality has seen both significant progress and enduring challenges. Since civil rights legislation banned overt discrimination in education and employment, American institutions and workplaces have become more diverse—although people of color are still underrepresented in the highest echelons of many professions. Black people have broken barriers and achieved recognition in various sectors.

The most historic "first" was the election of Barack Obama, a Democrat and the son of a Black Kenyan father and white American mother, as the nation's forty-fourth president in 2008 (see "Change

Antiracism demonstration in Charlottesville, August 12, 2018.
Erin Schaff / The New York Times / Redux

in 2008," p. 151). President Obama's victory was celebrated as a major milestone of racial advancement. Yet, it also stoked resentment among many white Americans, who perceived him as a threat to their privilege and power.[117] This sentiment, in part, fueled the surge of white supremacist groups and hate crimes.[118]

During the 2010s, Americans continued grappling with racial inequalities. As a result of centuries of discrimination, systemic racism is deeply embedded in all facets of American life, from social interactions to the policies and practices of businesses and institutions. Black Americans fare worse than their white counterparts in most life indicators, including economic, health, employment, education, and voting access. And many disparities are wider today than during the civil rights era (see fig.).[119]

The 2015 murder of nine Black church members by a white supremacist in Charleston, South Carolina, prompted a reexamination of Confederate memorials, most of which were erected during the Jim Crow era as symbols of white supremacy and the Lost Cause mythology. Virginia, home to more Confederate symbols than any other state, became the epicenter of debates about their removal.[120] In the summer of 2017, white supremacist groups staged rallies in Charlottesville and clashed with antiracist counter-protesters. This deadly violence shocked the world, and President Donald Trump's remarks that there "were very fine people on both sides" further enflamed tensions (see entry on Zyahna Bryant, p. 159).[121]

Another contentious issue involves the disproportionate killing of unarmed Black people by law enforcement. Black Americans are nearly three times more likely to die at the hands of police than white people.[122] Black Lives Matter (BLM) emerged in 2013 as a hashtag proclaiming Black humanity in the face of societal devaluation. It has evolved into a global activist network that organizes demonstrations and advocates for criminal justice reform. The violence that erupted at some protests provoked criticism of BLM and a harsh police response, further eroding relations between communities of color and law enforcement.[123]

The year 2020 brought about a national reckoning on the painful legacies of slavery, segregation, and white supremacy. The coronavirus pandemic and the groundswell of social justice protests following the police murder of George Floyd laid bare the country's racial inequalities. And debates over how to respond to these crises enflamed an already bitterly divided nation during a presidential election year. Although America's racial problems can feel intractable, there are signs of change. Current events have fostered a new awareness of systemic racism and a renewed determination to make meaningful change. The 400-year-long fight for equity for all Americans continues.

FIGHTING SCHOOL SEGREGATION

BARBARA JOHNS POWELL (1935–1991)

"It wasn't fair that we had such a poor facility, equipment, etc., when our white counterparts enjoyed science laboratories, a huge facility, separate gym dept. etc."[124]

In April 1951, high school junior Barbara Johns (later Powell) led a student protest that helped dismantle the "separate but equal" foundation of school segregation.[125] During Jim Crow, educational inequities were rampant as white schools received about four times more funding per student than Black schools. For instance, to deal with overcrowding, Johns's school—Robert Russa Moton High in Farmville, Prince Edward County—held classes in tar-paper shacks with no plumbing and poor heating. Moton also lacked many of the resources available at Farmville's white high school.

Fed up with such deplorable conditions, Johns organized a two-week student strike to demand change. She and fellow students also convinced Spottswood Robinson III and Oliver Hill, Sr.—attorneys for the National Association for the Advancement of Colored People (NAACP) and Virginia's leading civil rights lawyers—to take up their fight. It was a fortuitous moment as the NAACP was developing a legal campaign to challenge the constitutionality of segregation in the courts. Johns was one of 117 student plaintiffs in *Davis et al.* v. *County School Board of Prince Edward County*. As the case progressed, she went to live with family in Alabama because of threats on her life.

When it reached the U.S. Supreme Court, the *Davis* case was bundled with four other cases from Delaware, South Carolina, Kansas, and the District of Columbia to become *Brown* v. *Board of Education of Topeka, Kansas*.[126] In its landmark decision rendered May 17, 1954, the court declared school segregation unconstitutional, ruling that "in

Robert Shetterly, *Barbara Johns*, 2010, oil on canvas.
© Robert Shetterly / Americans Who Tell The Truth

Barbara Johns

It was time that Negroes were treated equally with whites, time
that they had a decent school, time for the students themselves to do
something about it.
There wasn't any fear. I just felt — this is your moment.
Seize it!

the field of public education the doctrine of 'separate but equal' has no place. Separate educational facilities are inherently unequal."

As momentous as the *Brown* decision was, opposition was intense and implementation difficult. Virginia's white political establishment and many white citizens fought desegregation with a highly coordinated campaign known as Massive Resistance—which became a model for other Southern states. Opponents to integration accused the federal government of infringing on states' rights and individual liberties and claimed that integration would lead to "the destruction of our culture."[127] Beginning in 1956, the state government cut funding to or closed schools that tried to integrate, created student placement boards that effectively maintained segregation, and launched sham investigations to intimidate Black plaintiffs and their lawyers. When these obstructionist

NAACP attorneys Spottswood Robinson (left) and Oliver Hill (right) with students George Leakes and Elaine Bowen in court in Virginia, 1953.
Library of Congress

measures were declared unconstitutional in 1959, Prince Edward County closed its public schools for five years rather than integrate. Other districts delayed implementing desegregation until a 1968 Supreme Court decision, *Charles Green* v. *County School Board of New Kent County, Virginia*, ordered the end to such tactics.[128]

Although Barbara Johns's goal of equal educational opportunities for all students remains elusive today, *Brown* v. *Board of Education* was a watershed for ending legal segregation in America. It also laid the foundation for subsequent legislation banning discrimination in education for women (Title IX, 1972) and for people with mental and physical disabilities (1975).

Fred Seibel, *Another Merrimac and Monitor,* cartoon about Virginia's Massive Resistance published in the *Richmond-Times Dispatch*, September 2, 1958.

Courtesy of Special Collections, University of Virginia Library

During the 1950s and '60s, Virginia was a central battleground in the long, contentious fight to end segregation in America's public schools. The National Association for the Advancement of Colored People (NAACP), which spearheaded the legal fight, filed more lawsuits in the Commonwealth than in any other state. And Virginia's Massive Resistance served as a model for other states opposed to desegregation.

Students protesting school closings in Farmville, Prince Edward County, July 1963.
Richmond Times-Dispatch

DECISIVE MOMENTS INCLUDE:

1954

Brown v. Board of Education
Landmark U.S. Supreme Court decision declaring that separate schools are unconstitutional; overturns the doctrine of "separate but equal" established by *Plessy* v. *Ferguson* (1896).

1955

Brown II
Follow-up ruling declares that desegregation must occur "with all deliberate speed." Southern states respond with a range of delaying tactics.

1956

Massive Resistance begins
Virginia's General Assembly calls for a campaign of Massive Resistance to defy the federal order to desegregate schools.

1958

School closures begin
Virginia's Governor Lindsay Almond, Jr., begins closing schools that violate his executive order blocking desegregation. Parents of white and Black students scramble to provide makeshift schools.

1959

Massive Resistance officially ends
The courts declare Governor Almond's order illegal. Some districts begin to desegregate, but opposition continues. Prince Edward County closes its public schools rather than integrate: many white students attend a private academy, many Black students lose years of education.

1964

Griffin v. School Board of Prince Edward County
U.S. Supreme Court rules that denying students a public education is unconstitutional and orders Prince Edward County to reopen its schools.

1968

Green v. County School Board of New Kent County
U.S. Supreme Court decision ends bureaucratic delays and obstructionist tactics against desegregation. Justice William Brennan privately notes that "the traffic light [on school integration] will have changed from *Brown* to *Green*."

TO TODAY

The 1970s and '80s saw the rise and fall of controversial busing programs to achieve racial balance, as well as "white flight" from cities and declining investment in urban schools. Today, many schools in Virginia and throughout the United States are as racially segregated as they were in 1954.

CIVIL RIGHTS LEADER

WYATT TEE WALKER (1929–2018)

The Rev. Dr. Wyatt Tee Walker was an icon of the civil rights movement, first in Virginia and then on the national stage. Raised in New Jersey, he attended Virginia Union University in Richmond, receiving his Master of Divinity in 1953. During his studies, he met another seminarian—the Rev. Dr. Martin Luther King, Jr. The two became close friends and fellow freedom fighters. From 1953 to 1959, Walker was the pastor of Gillfield Baptist Church in Petersburg, one of the oldest Black churches in the country. He also served as president of the local chapter of the National Association for the Advancement of Colored People (NAACP) and state director of the Congress of Racial Equality (CORE), and founded the Petersburg Improvement Association, which worked to desegregate the city's facilities. As he argued,

> segregation is a sin against personality. It scars not only the soul of the *segregated*, but also the *segregator*. It refutes the dignity and worth of every person.[129]

Walker led a range of protest activities in Petersburg and around Virginia, while also training activists in the principles of nonviolent resistance. He championed direct action—marches, boycotts, and sit-ins—to effect change. "I was convinced," he said of this strategy, "that the way to make changes in the white community was . . . to mess with the money; and you had to make it inconvenient."[130] One such protest was a sit-in at the Petersburg Public Library in March 1960. After using the whites-only entrance, Walker tried to check

Wyatt Tee Walker (left) training activists for sit-in harassment in Petersburg, Virginia, 1960.

Photo by Howard Sochurek / The LIFE Premium Collection via Getty Images / Getty Images

[above left] Wyatt Tee Walker
(right), Martin Luther King,
Jr., and Joseph Lowery at
the SCLC conference in
Richmond, 1963.
Richmond Times-Dispatch

[above right] Program for a
mass meeting, Virginia State
Unit of the SCLC, signed by
Martin Luther King, Jr., Wyatt
Tee Walker, Ralph Abernathy,
and other leaders, March
28, 1962.
VMHC, Purchased with funds
provided by L. Dudley Walker

out a biography of Confederate hero Robert E. Lee. Although he was
arrested—his first of seventeen arrests for civil disobedience—the
library integrated later that year.

Martin Luther King, Jr., who considered Walker to have "the keenest
mind in the civil rights movement," tapped him to be the first executive
director of the Southern Christian Leadership Conference (SCLC).[131] As
King's right-hand man from 1960 to 1964, Walker developed fundraising
strategies, coordinated with civil rights groups around the South, and
organized several major demonstrations, including the Birmingham
Campaign in Alabama in the spring of 1963. This series of marches
and boycotts became a turning point in the movement because of
the economic impact on local businesses and the international outcry
in response to images of police attacking dignified, peaceful Black
protesters with clubs, dogs, and high-pressure water hoses. Walker also
planned the March on Washington of August 1963, during which King
delivered his "I Have a Dream" speech.

Working both on the front lines and behind the scenes of the civil
rights movement, Walker regularly faced death threats. Yet, he and
other activists persisted because "we were committed to the ideals
of freedom and equality for every American citizen."[132] Their courage,
determination, and sacrifice inspired change in laws and public opinion.

In 1967, Walker became pastor of Harlem's Canaan Baptist
Church in New York City. During his thirty-seven-year ministry, he
rose to international prominence as he continued fighting for racial
equity, economic and educational opportunities, and human rights for
oppressed people around the world.

The civil rights movement culminated in key legislation that prohibited race-based discrimination and guaranteed voting rights and equal opportunities for Black people. The most sweeping civil rights legislation since the Reconstruction era, these new federal laws profoundly changed American society by promising legal equality for all Americans.

1964

Civil Rights Act

- Outlawed "discrimination or segregation on the ground of race, color, religion, or national origin" in public places and employment
- Passed Congress after intense debate and the longest filibuster in U.S. history
- Later expanded to protect women, the elderly, and people with disabilities

1965

Voting Rights Act

- Made it illegal to use literacy tests and other discriminatory measures to restrict voting
- Section V required certain states that historically disenfranchised Black voters—including Virginia—to obtain federal clearance for any changes to voting laws
- By 1968, Black voter registration had increased by 67 percent[133]

1968

Civil Rights Act (commonly called the Fair Housing Act)

- Banned discrimination in the sale, rental, and financing of housing based on race, religion, national origin, and sex

ARE WE BACKTRACKING?

2013

***Shelby County* v. *Holder,* U.S. Supreme Court decision**

- Struck down formula for determining which states are covered under Section V of the 1965 Voting Rights Act
- Led to a wave of new voting restrictions—including voter ID laws and voter roll purges—that disproportionately affect minority and low-income voters

[above] President Lyndon B. Johnson shaking hands with Dr. Martin Luther King, Jr., and others after the Voting Rights Act signing ceremony, August 6, 1965.
LBJ Presidential Library / Photo by Yoichi Okamoto

[left] Civil rights protesters outside the White House, March 12, 1965.
Library of Congress

HIDDEN FIGURE

GLADYS WEST (B. 1930)

"Her competence, not her color, defined her."
– Dr. Jim Colvard, former technical director, Naval Surface Weapons
Center Dahlgren Division[134]

A trailblazing mathematician, Dr. Gladys West was integral to the development of GPS (global positioning system)—technology that has transformed modern life. Like other Black female "hidden figures" in the defense and aerospace industries, she had to overcome the dual, intersectional challenges of racism and sexism.[135] West's career presents a testament not only to her individual talents, but also to the significant contributions made by Black Americans in professions that had previously been closed to them due to segregation and discrimination.

Born Gladys Brown in Dinwiddie County, she was determined from a young age to escape the jobs typically available to poor rural Black Virginians—working in the fields or tobacco factories. Realizing that she "had to get an education to get out," she became valedictorian of her high school in order to win a scholarship to Virginia State University.[136] After earning a Bachelor's (1952) and a Master's degree (1955), and short stints as a math teacher, West got a job in January 1956 as a mathematician at the U.S. Naval Proving Ground—later Naval Surface Weapons Center. As the Cold War and space race were heating up, this naval base conducted research and development for the U.S. military in weapons and computing technology.

Gladys West in her office at
the Naval Surface Weapons
Center, Dahlgren, 1977.
Gladys and Ira West

When she arrived at Dahlgren, West was one of only four Black people in the lab. This small group included one other woman and Ira West, who became her husband. Gladys West keenly felt the pressures of breaking barriers. At a time when many Americans assumed that Black women were incapable of advanced intellectual pursuits, she "made sure to work twice as hard as our white counterparts." She also recalled, "I carried that load around, thinking that I had to be the best . . . to set an example for other people who were coming behind me, especially women."[137]

During her forty-two-year career at Dahlgren, West specialized in the field of satellite geodesy, the science of measuring the shape and size of the earth from space. Her work involved creating algorithms and programs for analyzing satellite data using early supercomputers. She contributed to numerous projects, including GPS in the 1960s and '70s and SEASAT, which began in 1978 and became the first satellite to map oceans from space (see fig.).

West earned respect from her peers and accolades within her field, but outside recognition as a "hidden figure of GPS" came much later—long after her 1998 retirement. In 2018 she was inducted into the Air Force Space and Missile Pioneers Hall of Fame. Still committed to education, she earned a Ph.D. in 2000, and Gladys and Ira West established a scholarship to help Virginia students pursuing mathematics and other STEM degrees.

[below left] Diagram from Gladys West, "SEASAT Satellite Radar Altimetry Data Processing System," Naval Surface Weapons Center Report, May 1981.
VMHC, Gift of Carolyn W. Oglesby

[below right] State Senator Bill DeSteph and Gladys West at Virginia's General Assembly recognition ceremony, March 1, 2018.
Mike Morones / The Free Lance-Star

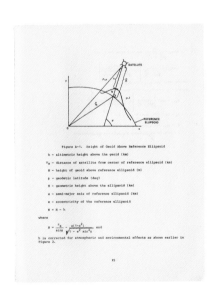

CHAMPION ON AND OFF THE COURT

ARTHUR ASHE, JR. (1943–1993)

P rofessional sports have long been more than just athletic contests: they also serve as a proving ground for American ideals of equality, fairness, and a democratic society of merit-based success. As Black athletes began crossing the color line in the mid-20th century—perhaps most famously Jackie Robinson in major league baseball in 1947—they helped advance the cause of racial justice.

Arthur Ashe began his remarkable career on Richmond's segregated tennis courts. At age ten, he drew the attention of Dr. Robert Walter Johnson of Lynchburg, a pioneering coach of Black players, including Althea Gibson. Under Johnson's mentorship, Ashe trained and learned good sportsmanship and respectability—necessary skills for entering what was long considered a lily-white country club sport. He gained national attention, as well as the opportunity to compete with white players, during college at the University of California, Los Angeles (UCLA).

During the 1960s and '70s, Ashe was one of the top-ranked players in the world. In 1963, he became the first Black person to make the U.S. team for the Davis Cup, an international team competition. This was one of many "firsts" in men's tennis and one he considered more important than his individual victories. "Winning a place on our national team [marked] my ultimate triumph over all those people who had opposed my career . . . in the name of segregation."[138] He was also the first Black man to win the U.S. Open (1968), Australian Open (1970), and Wimbledon (1975)—all Grand Slam titles—as well as the first to be inducted into the International Tennis Hall of Fame (1985). Heart problems forced him to retire from competition in 1980.

Ashe became even more famous off the court as a champion of human rights. When South Africa refused to let him play in the country in 1969, he became a vocal anti-apartheid activist. He also protested the U.S. government's treatment of Haitian refugees. He supported a

[above] Arthur Ashe's Davis Cup ring, which he won as a member of the championship team, 1970.
VMHC

[right] Arthur Ashe holding the Wimbledon trophy after defeating Jimmy Connors, July 5, 1975.
Associated Press

Arthur Ashe being arrested outside the South African Embassy in Washington, D.C., during an anti-apartheid protest, 1985.

Associated Press

range of other causes, including youth sports and education and, after he contracted the disease through a blood transfusion, AIDS advocacy. His three-volume *A Hard Road to Glory* (1988) was a groundbreaking study of the history of Black athletes.

Throughout his career, Ashe earned acclaim for his unflappable grace under pressure—grace he maintained during the highs and lows of a match and in the face of daily racism, which he described as "the heaviest burden I have had to bear."[139] Some people criticized Ashe as too moderate on Black civil rights, particularly in comparison to other athlete-activists, such as Muhammad Ali, who refused to fight in the Vietnam War, and Tommie Smith and John Carlos, who gave the Black Power salute at the 1968 Olympics. Yet, Ashe's reserved manner allowed him to break barriers and effect change. The mixing of sports and politics remains controversial today, as seen in debates surrounding football players kneeling during the national anthem and other actions taken to protest the killing of Black people by police and systemic racism.

POLITICAL FIRSTS

L. DOUGLAS WILDER (B. 1931)

Poster from Douglas Wilder's state senate campaign, in which he won a plurality of votes against two white candidates, 1969.

VMHC

The victories of the civil rights era fueled increased civic participation among Black Americans as both voters and officeholders— transforming Virginia's political landscape. From 1964 to 1968, the number of Black Southerners casting ballots rose by approximately 67 percent, due in large part to the Voting Rights Act of 1965 and concerted activism around voter registration.[140] A new generation of Black politicians also won office at local and state levels. In Virginia, Dr. William Ferguson Reid was elected to the House of Delegates in 1967 and L. Douglas Wilder to the State Senate in 1969, making them the first Black Americans to serve in the General Assembly since the late 1800s (see entry on Peter Jacob Carter, p. 104).

A Richmond native and grandson of slaves, Douglas Wilder grew up under segregation. He attended Virginia Union University and fought in the Korean War, receiving a Bronze Star. *Brown* v. *Board of Education* (1954), which desegregated public schools, inspired Wilder to become a lawyer so that he could be part of the change ushered in by this watershed Supreme Court decision.[141] After earning his degree at Howard University and establishing a successful legal practice in Richmond, he set his sights on politics.

Wilder's entry into public service was motivated, in part, by his frustration with solidarity politics in which Black organizations pushed their community to vote as a bloc for a particular ticket. Wilder argued that voters should focus on the issues, stating, "Many candidates just assumed that African American voters were . . . hordes of dumb cattle going through the motions of exercising a constitutional guarantee rather than being seriously affected by their country's future." In 1969, he ran as a Democrat for the Virginia Senate with the campaign message that he wanted to represent "all the people, not just *my* people." Although this position angered some in the Black community, Wilder won the seat with a coalition of Black and white voters.[142]

In one of his first acts as a state senator, he denounced the state anthem, "Carry Me Back to Old Virginny," a racially offensive song that romanticized slavery. This willingness to take a bold and controversial stance was a hallmark of Wilder's career. During five terms in the Virginia Senate, he advanced legislation dealing with discrimination, fair housing, and juvenile criminal reform, among other issues.

Wilder achieved more political firsts. His 1985 election as lieutenant governor made him the first Black statewide officeholder. For this campaign, he visited every county in the Commonwealth, including predominantly white regions, to gain support. In 1989, he successfully ran for governor, becoming the first elected Black governor in U.S. history and the only one until 2006.[143] During his term (1990–1994), he won praise for his sound fiscal management during an economic recession. In his later career, Wilder taught at Virginia Commonwealth University and returned briefly to politics as Richmond's first popularly elected mayor (2004–2008); previously, the City Council appointed the mayor. His legacy of building diverse coalitions made Wilder a powerful force in Virginia civic life and a national model for other politicians.

[above left] Inauguration of Douglas Wilder as Virginia's governor, with Lieutenant Governor Donald Beyer and Attorney General Mary Sue Terry, January 13, 1990.
Richmond Times-Dispatch

[above right] Governor Douglas Wilder's cowboy boots decorated with the seal of the Commonwealth of Virginia, made by Lucchese, 1990s.
VMHC, Gift of the Honorable L. Douglas Wilder

Presidential candidate Barack Obama at a campaign rally in Virginia Beach, October 30, 2008.
Getty Images

Virginia played a pivotal role in the historic election of President Barack Obama—the nation's first Black president—in 2008 and again in 2012. This state, which had voted Republican in presidential elections since 1968, turned from "red" to "blue" and helped deliver an electoral victory to the Democratic candidate. President Obama's momentous achievement resonated across the globe. It took on special significance in Virginia given the Commonwealth's centrality in American history as:

- the place where American democracy *and* American slavery began

- the crucible for the ideal that "all men are created equal"

- the capital of the Confederacy

- a national symbol of Jim Crow segregation and oppression.

MUSICAL PIONEER

MISSY ELLIOTT (B. 1971)

Across the centuries, African American music has profoundly shaped American music through spirituals, jazz, rock 'n' roll, and R&B. In recent decades, rap and hip-hop have taken this influence global. Originating in the 1970s in Black urban neighborhoods as a form of social protest and an expressive outlet for marginalized groups, hip-hop has evolved into a worldwide cultural phenomenon with multiple styles and regional flavors. The Virginia Beach area has been a breeding ground for hip-hop talent, including Teddy Riley, DeVanté Swing, Pharrell Williams, Timothy "Timbaland" Mosley, and Missy "Misdemeanor" Elliott.

Born Melissa Arnette Elliott in Portsmouth, Missy Elliott has been revolutionizing the genre since the early 1990s as a singer, songwriter, producer, and fashion icon. One of the bestselling female rappers of all time and a four-time Grammy winner, she became the first female hip-hop artist, and only the third rapper, inducted into the Songwriters Hall of Fame (2019). Elliott began her career in the R&B group Sista and as part of the Swing Mob collective, earning her earliest acclaim as a songwriter and producer. With Timbaland, her childhood friend and creative partner, she crafted tracks for many of the hottest acts, including Aaliyah, Ginuwine, Whitney Houston, Destiny's Child, and others. She continues to work collaboratively with artists such as Pharrell, Lizzo, and Dua Lipa.

Elliott's debut solo album, *Supa Dupa Fly* (1997), catapulted her to the top of the charts and established her status as an utterly original creative force. Critics praised her sophisticated samplings, skewed tempos, and futuristic aesthetic. This album and its videos also presented a new vision of Black femininity in a genre that generally pigeonholed women as either masculinized tough guys or hypersexualized vixens. In her video for "The Rain," for example, Elliott's appearance shifts between masculine and feminine—and even cyborgian. She also challenges white, heteronormative ideals of female

Track-suit jacket from the "Respect M.E." line that Missy Elliott created with Adidas, about 2004.
VMHC, Purchased through the James H. Willcox, Jr. Fund

Cover of *Vibe*, featuring Virginia's hip-hop talents Timbaland, Missy Elliott, and The Neptunes (Chad Hugo and Pharrell Williams), September 2003.

VMHC

beauty by donning an inflated black suit that emphasizes her curves. Similarly, close-ups of her mouth through a fish-eye lens exaggerate her lips in a sly reference to historical caricatures of Black people.[144]

Elliott was the dominant female hip-hop artist of the late 1990s and 2000s—and the only one to have six platinum albums. Her feminist message of sexual empowerment and body positivity—she raps "I've got a cute face / chubby waist / thick legs in shape / rump shaking both ways / make you do a double take" in "Lose Control" (2005)—has been immensely influential across the music industry. She is also renowned for her innovative use of sounds, as in "Work It" (2002): the lyric "I put my thing down, flip it and reverse it" is literally reversed to become non-sensical speech, pure noise.

Elliott's impact on contemporary music has paved the way for other female superstars like Beyoncé and Nicki Minaj. "Throw It Back" (2019), one of Elliott's latest releases, declares her legendary status:

I'll show you how I do it
Show you how it's done
Don't look for another Missy
'Cause there'll be no 'nother one.

Missy Elliott at the Essence
Festival, New Orleans, 2018.

ENVIRONMENTAL JUSTICE ACTIVIST

QUEEN ZAKIA SHABAZZ (B. 1960)

"Everyone deserves to live in a healthy environment, breathe clean air, drink clean water and access affordable, clean energy. Unfortunately, that is not the reality for many Virginians."[145]

Systemic racism infiltrates all aspects of life, including the air that we breathe. People of color and low-income families often bear the brunt of harm from environmental toxins and climate change. Industrial zones, landfills, power plants, and other polluters are frequently placed in or near non-white neighborhoods—the result of longstanding patterns of race-based discrimination in residential segregation, financial disinvestment, and political disempowerment in these communities. A landmark study in 2007 found "race to be more important than socioeconomic status in predicting the location of the nation's commercial hazardous waste facilities." Another racial disparity is that Black children are five times more likely to be exposed to lead poisoning than white children.[146] Environmental racism, as this phenomenon is called, also extends to policy-making and regulatory enforcement, as well as to disparities in infrastructure and services—like access to healthy foods.

For Queen Zakia Shabazz, who likes to say she is "from Earth," the effects of environmental racism hit home in 1996.[147] Her son, a toddler at the time, got lead poisoning from old lead-based paint in their Richmond house. In children, exposure to lead causes irreversible brain damage, physical and developmental delays, and other problems, and sometimes death. Frustrated by the lack of help from municipal and medical authorities, Shabazz became an expert on and grassroots activist against lead poisoning, and she founded United Parents Against Lead (UPAL). This organization promotes public awareness, assists families, works with government agencies to set policies, funds lead

Queen Zakia Shabazz, 2006.
Photo: Garrie Rouse

[above left] Logo of the Virginia Environmental Justice Collaborative (VEJC).
Courtesy of the VEJC

[above right] March to protect Union Hill, a historic Black community in Buckingham County, from becoming the site of a natural-gas compressor station, 2018.
Courtesy of the Sierra Club Virginia Chapter

remediation projects, and fights for safe housing and schools. One lobbying campaign to improve lead-testing standards ran with the slogan "Stop using our children as lead detectors." In 2004, Shabazz led UPAL in securing a $2 million Department of Housing and Urban Development (HUD) grant to test 120 homes and perform remediation in eighty in Richmond and Petersburg—two cities with large Black communities and large stocks of old buildings. In the wake of the water crisis in Flint, Michigan, in 2015, she has also fought for testing, prevention, and remediation in Richmond-area elementary schools.

Since 2017, Shabazz has served as the coordinator of the Virginia Environmental Justice Collaborative (VEJC), a coalition of thirty-five organizations working across the Commonwealth. The VEJC helped prevent the construction of a natural-gas compressor station in Union Hill, a historic Black community founded by freedmen after the Civil War. At the state level, the VEJC also lobbied the governor to establish the Virginia Council on Environmental Justice and the General Assembly to pass the Virginia Environmental Justice Act (2020), which makes protecting "all people regardless of race, color, national origin, income, faith, or disability" a priority in environmental policies and regulations. Recognizing the interconnectedness of systemic racism and environmental justice, Queen Zakia Shabazz continues to amplify the voices of vulnerable communities and to advocate for safe, equitable, and sustainable lives for all Virginians.

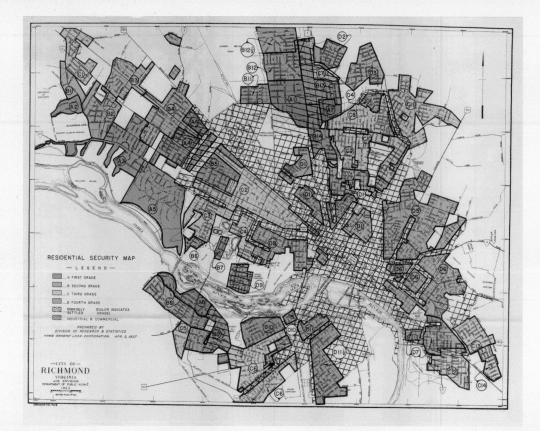

Despite the remarkable progress toward Black equality in America, true equity remains elusive. People of color face systemic racism and socioeconomic inequalities in all facets of life. Many of these persistent disparities are rooted in the legacies of Jim Crow. For instance, residential segregation—whether by legal ordinance or social custom—jeopardized the economic growth of Black communities across America, trapping many Black neighborhoods in cycles of poverty and decay.

The Federal Housing Administration, created during the Great Depression to help families keep their homes, worsened the effects of segregation through "redlining." This practice designated certain districts—usually Black—too risky to insure mortgages. In subsequent decades, lower rates of investment, infrastructure, and home ownership in these neighborhoods led to their economic decline, making them primary targets for demolition to make way for highways and other "development" projects.

In addition, environmental racism also disproportionately impacts low-income people and people of color. They often live in places that are the most vulnerable to the effects of climate change and the closest to industrial and other polluters that expose residents to toxins in the air, water, and soil.

[above] Home Owners Loan Corporation, Map of Richmond, showing redlining with Black neighborhoods marked in red, 1937.
Courtesy of Redlining Richmond, Digital Scholarship Lab, University of Richmond

THE RISING GENERATION

ZYAHNA BRYANT (B. 2000)

"Before we can heal as a community, and as a nation, we must truly reckon with our past and call out white supremacy in all of its forms."[148]

Charlottesville native Zyahna Bryant represents the rising generation of social justice activists fighting against systemic racism. Her activism began at a young age, when she organized a march in response to the innocent verdict for the Florida man who killed Black teenager Trayvon Martin in 2012. She joined Black Lives Matter and formed the Black Student Union at Charlottesville High School.

In 2016, for a school assignment on "how to make a change," Bryant decided to start a petition to remove Charlottesville's monument to Robert E. Lee and change the name of Lee Park where it stood. Every time she passed the statue, she wrote, "I am reminded over and over again of the pain of my ancestors and all of the fighting that they had to go through for us to be where we are now."[149] Bryant's petition garnered hundreds of signatures, prompted the city council to establish a special commission, and sparked a community dialogue on the meaning and legacy of Confederate symbols.

In response to the city's decision to remove the statue, white supremacist groups targeted Charlottesville for a series of demonstrations during the summer of 2017. The Unite the Right rallies on August 11–12 stunned the nation with scenes of marchers bearing torches and spewing Nazi slogans, and of their violent clashes with counter-protesters—resulting in the death of Heather Heyer, an antiracist protester. These events signaled a resurgence of white supremacist activity in recent years—a resurgence in reaction to Barack Obama's presidency. (At the time of writing, the fate of Charlottesville's Lee statue remains tied up in the courts. Lee Park is now named Emancipation Park.)

Zyahna Bryant, 2018.
Matt Eich

Currently a student at the University of Virginia, Bryant continues to fight for racial justice. Her work as an activist and community organizer has been widely recognized. Among her many accolades are the Student Stowe Prize from the Harriet Beecher Stowe Center, the Princeton Prize in Race Relations from Princeton University, and the Yale Basset Award for Community Engagement from Yale University. In 2019, Governor Ralph Northam appointed her to the Virginia African American Advisory Board, which addresses issues impacting Black communities around the Commonwealth. She also mentors young activists.

Bryant admits that confronting racism in America is uncomfortable, but necessary for us all to do. Her message is simple, yet impactful—educate yourself on the issues, elevate marginalized voices, and call out injustices wherever you see them. As she wrote in a recent op-ed reflecting on George Floyd's death and related protests in 2020:

> It is imperative that we have a conversation about where we, as a society, go from here. It seems there is an overwhelming expectation that Black activists and organizers will say something profound about Black death, but what I have to offer is not some profound truth but a simple request: take action.[150]

[above left] Spent tear gas canister used by police to disperse demonstrators protesting the KKK rally in Charlottesville, July 8, 2017.
Courtesy of Special Collections, University of Virginia Library

[above right] Zyahna Bryant and Charlottesville Mayor Nikuya Walker collecting soil for the National Lynching Memorial, 2018.
© Eze Amos

SMALL STEPS, BIG IMPACT

BELLEN WOODARD (B. 2010)

When she was in third grade, Bellen Woodard was asked by another student at her Loudoun County school to pass the "skin-colored crayon." She understood that her classmate wanted the peach crayon based on the typical use of peach hues to depict white skin and on societal assumptions that whiteness is the norm. (Crayola labeled its "Peach" crayon "Flesh" until 1962.) Yet, this presumption bothered her because it did not reflect her own skin tone—she felt "disincluded." Woodard decided to respond to future requests by asking "Which color do you want?" This simple question is quite astute: it prompts deliberation—disrupting the assumption that there is only one skin-colored crayon.[151]

Woodard has been working ever since to foster change. She started with conversations in her classroom to address racial biases embedded in language, not only for crayons, but also for race in general. For instance, when a white classmate described his skin color as "sand" and Woodard's as "dirt," she pointed out the derogatory associations of the word he used to label Blackness.

In 2019, at age nine, Woodard also founded Bellen's More Than Peach Project with the mission of providing more inclusive crayons to kids. Using her own savings, she created coloring kits with a sketchpad and crayons and colored pencils in a diverse array of skin tones. Her initial goal was to distribute kits to students in her county, but the project quickly took off and expanded across the country. More Than Peach now sells kits online and offers its own branded products, including a multicultural crayon palette with twelve skin-toned colors custom-designed by Woodard (see fig.). Proceeds from sales fund donations to kids and schools with a need.

The project's celebration of diversity and inclusivity has resonated with classrooms and families around the world. One woman related

Bellen Woodard, 2020.
Courtesy of the Woodard Family

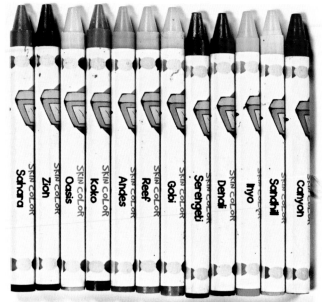

how, when her seven-year-old grandson saw the More Than Peach crayons, he pointed to the Serengeti color and exclaimed, "That's my Dad!" The grandmother continued, "I teared up . . . just imagining how important these crayons will be to kids worldwide."[152] Woodard has also garnered international media coverage and acclaim for her activism. In 2020, she received the Rising Star Award from the National Coalition of Black Women, was one of five finalists in the Time / Nickelodeon Kid of the Year award, and was an honoree of the Anti-Defamation League's Concert Against Hate.

Her work is critically important given that children begin showing racial bias between ages three and five. The famous "doll tests" conducted by social psychologists Drs. Mamie and Kenneth Clark in the 1940s demonstrated how Black children internalized the racist prejudices of Jim Crow by being more likely to prefer white baby dolls and to ascribe negative traits to Black ones (see fig.). With More Than Peach, Bellen Woodard tackles racial bias in childhood—allowing kids to see themselves represented in crayons and promoting the beauty of all skin colors. This young crayon activist will no doubt continue changing the world to make a better future.

[above left] Dr. Kenneth Clark observing a child playing with Black and white dolls. Photograph by Gordon Parks, *Untitled*, Harlem, New York, 1947.
Courtesy of and copyright The Gordon Parks Foundation

[above right] Bellen's More Than Peach multicultural crayon palette, 2020.
Courtesy of Bellen's More Than Peach Project

EPILOGUE:
TO BE DETERMINED

"For too long we've been blind to the way past injustices continue to shape the present. Perhaps we see that now. Perhaps this tragedy causes us to ask some tough questions about how we can permit so many of our children to languish in poverty, or attend dilapidated schools. . . . Perhaps it causes us to examine what we're doing to cause some of our children to hate."
– President Barack Obama, June 26, 2015[153]

President Barack Obama uttered these words of reckoning after a white supremacist killed nine Black worshippers at Emanuel African Methodist Episcopal Church in Charleston, South Carolina. Similar calls for change have followed other recent events across the United States, including the numerous instances of an unarmed Black person dying at the hands of police, the white supremacist rallies in Charlottesville in 2017, and the global pandemic and wave of racial justice protests of 2020.

On one hand, these latest demands for a national reckoning on race seem too familiar to contain any hope for change in America's status quo on race relations. Yet, on the other hand, 2020 feels decidedly different. It really does seem like the United States is at an inflection point on race.

This sense comes, in part, from the scope of the pandemic's impact and the horror of George Floyd's death. These events have brought racial inequalities to the forefront of national discourse. They have also stripped away the blinders of many white people to the daily biases and risks faced by their Black neighbors. The increased awareness of systemic racism—what it is and how it operates—has spurred widespread efforts to fight it. The level of social justice activism sweeping the nation has not been seen since the civil rights era. To redress past injustices, many communities are working on criminal justice and other reforms, and

many companies and institutions are committing to diversity, equity, and inclusion (DEI) initiatives.

This book was largely written during the fall of 2020—too early to assess the outcome of this call for racial reckoning. But we do know from history that change is hard won and often slow, yet possible. And there are signs that change is happening. The United States elected Kamala Harris as its first female vice president and the first person of African and Asian descent to hold that office. In Richmond, just blocks from the Virginia Museum of History & Culture, Confederate monuments have been dismantled and Virginia's state government is pushing legislative reforms on racial equity issues.

Ultimately, we hope that *Determined* prompts you to ask tough questions and to understand how past injustices have shaped our present society. This book looks back over 400 years, but it also has an eye to the future. This history of the Black struggle for equality is marked by advances and setbacks—both of which provide useful lessons for fostering change and recognizing patterns of backlash. After encountering the remarkable stories of Black courage, resistance, and fortitude contained herein, we hope that you are determined to continue the fight for equality for all people.

Artist Dustin Klein's projection of an image of George Floyd on the Robert E. Lee Monument in Richmond, June 6, 2020.
2020 / Scott Elmquist / Virginia-Pilot Archives / TNS

ENDNOTES

1   Martin Luther King, Jr., "I've Been to the Mountaintop," address delivered at Bishop Charles Mason Temple, Memphis, Tenn., April 3, 1968. The Martin Luther King, Jr., Research and Education Institute, Stanford University, https://kinginstitute.stanford.edu/king-papers/documents/ive-been-mountaintop-address-delivered-bishop-charles-mason-temple.

2   James Baldwin, "As Much of the Truth as One Can Bear," *New York Times*, January 14, 1962.

3   John Rolfe to Sir Edwin Sandys, January 1620, in *The Records of the Virginia Company of London*, ed. Susan Myra Kingsbury (Washington, D.C.: Government Printing Office, 1906–35), 3: 243; excerpts of this letter are also available online at *Encyclopedia Virginia*, last modified December 7, 2020, https://encyclopediavirginia.org/entries/twenty-and-odd-negroes-an-excerpt-from-a-letter-from-john-rolfe-to-sir-edwin-sandys-1619-1620. Rolfe's letter describes the *White Lion* as a "Dutch man of Warr"; it was an English privateer carrying letters of marque from the Netherlands.

4   Philip Morgan, ed., *"Don't Grieve After Me": The Black Experience in Virginia, 1619–1986* (Hampton, Va.: Hampton University, 1986), 16.

5   Ira Berlin established this concept in *Many Thousands Gone: The First Two Centuries of Slavery in North America* (Cambridge, Mass.: Belknap Press of Harvard University Press, 1998), 8–9.

6   For more information on this subject, see Brendan Wolfe, "Free Blacks in Colonial Virginia," *Encyclopedia Virginia*, last modified December 7, 2020, https://encyclopediavirginia.org/entries/free-blacks-in-colonial-virginia.

7   The figures in this chart are adapted from U.S. Bureau of the Census, "Estimated Population of American Colonies: 1610 to 1780," Series Z 1–19, in "Colonial and Pre-Federal Statistics," chap. Z of *Historical Statistics of the United States, Colonial Times to 1970, Part 2*, Bicentennial Edition (Washington, D.C.: United States Bureau of the Census, 1975), 1168, https://www2.census.gov/prod2/statcomp/documents/CT1970p2-13.pdf.

8   Edmund S. Morgan, *American Slavery, American Freedom: The Ordeal of Colonial Virginia*, new ed. (New York: W. W. Norton & Company, 2003), 301.

9   Paul Musselwhite, Peter C. Mancall, and James Horn, eds., *Virginia 1619: Slavery and Freedom in the Making of English America* (Chapel Hill: University of North Carolina Press, 2019), 100–104.

10   For historical sources and recent scholarship on Angela and other First Arrivals, see James Horn, *1619: Jamestown and the Forging of American Democracy* (New York: Basic Books, 2018), chap. 3.

11   Equiano writes that he was born in the Eboe (Ibo) kingdom in his autobiography, but Vincent Carretta found that Equiano's birthplace is listed as "Carolina" in records from his service in the Royal Navy and his baptism in a London church. See Carretta, *Equiano, the African: Biography of a Self-Made Man* (Athens: University of Georgia Press, 2005), 2.

12   Olaudah Equiano, *The Interesting Narrative of the Life of Olaudah Equiano, Written by Himself* [1789], ed. Robert J. Allison, 2nd ed. (Boston: Bedford / St. Martin's, 2006), 66–67, 70, 71. Allison's introduction provides a good overview of Equiano's life and the significance of his autobiography.

13   The Trans-Atlantic Slave Trade Database provides the most comprehensive analysis of the slave trade: see *Slave Voyages: The Trans-Atlantic Slave Trade Database* v2.2.12 (Atlanta: Emory University, 2019), https://www.slavevoyages.org/voyage/database.

14   This census is transcribed in William Thorndale, "The Virginia Census of 1619 [1620]," *Magazine of Virginia Genealogy* 33 (Summer 1995): 168.

15   Transcript of the July 9, 1640, court case, in H. R. McIlwane, ed., *Minutes of the Council and General Court of Colonial Virginia 1622–1632, 1670–1676* (Richmond: Library of Virginia, 1924), 466.

16   Good sources on race and the law include Philip J. Schwarz, *Slave Laws in Virginia* (Athens: University of Georgia Press, 1996), and Jane Purcell Guild, *Black Laws of Virginia: A Summary of the Legislative Acts of Virginia concerning Negroes from Earliest Times to the Present* (Richmond: Whittet & Shepperson, 1936). The comprehensive record of Virginia laws is William Waller Hening, ed., *The Statutes at Large, Being a Collection of All of the Laws of Virginia, from the First Session of the Legislature, in the Year 1619*, 13 vols. (Richmond, Philadelphia, and New York, 1809–1823), available on the VAGenWeb website at http://vagenweb.org/hening/index.htm.

17   The surviving records of Elizabeth Key's lawsuit are transcribed in Warren M. Billings, ed., *The Old Dominion in the Seventeenth Century: A Documentary History of Virginia, 1606–1700*, rev. ed. (Chapel Hill: University of North Carolina Press, 2007), 195–99.

18   This essay draws on Taunya Lovell Banks, "Dangerous Woman: Elizabeth Key's Freedom Suit—Subjecthood and Racialized Identity in Seventeenth-Century Colonial Virginia," *Akron Law Review* 41 (2008): 799–837, and Brent Tarter, "Key, Elizabeth (fl. 1655–1660)," *Encyclopedia Virginia*, last modified February 12, 2021, https://encyclopediavirginia.org/entries/key-elizabeth-fl-1655-1660.

19   Hening, *The Statutes at Large*, 2:481, http://vagenweb.org/hening/vol02-23.htm.

20   Anthony S. Parent, Jr., *Foul Means: The Formation of a Slave Society in Virginia, 1660–1740* (Chapel Hill: University of North Carolina Press, 2003), 148.

21   "Punishment for a Negro Rebel," *William and Mary Quarterly* 10, 1st ser. (January 1902): 177–78.

22   This entry draws on Philip J. Schwarz, *Twice Condemned: Slaves and the Criminal Laws of Virginia, 1705–1865* (Baton Rouge: Louisiana State University Press, 1988), 80–81, and Parent, *Foul Means*.

23   Robert Carter to Robert Jones (Carter's senior estate manager), October 10, 1727, in Edmund Berkeley, Jr., "Robert Carter as Agricultural Manager: His Letters to Robert Jones, 1727–1729," *Virginia Magazine of History and Biography* 101 (1993): 280.

24   Declaration of Independence, Miscellaneous Papers of the Continental Congress, 1774–1789, National Archives, Washington, D.C., https://catalog.archives.gov/id/1419123.

25   James Madison, *Notes of Debates in the Federal Convention of 1787*, ed. Adrienne Koch (Athens: Ohio University Press, 1966), 295.

26   Douglas R. Egerton, *Death or Liberty: African Americans and Revolutionary America* (New York: Oxford University Press, 2009), 137. In 1806, the General Assembly passed new legislation requiring that newly manumitted Black people must leave the Commonwealth within twelve months.

27   An influential proponent of scientific racism, Thomas Jefferson detailed his views that Black people are "inferior to the whites in the endowments both of body and mind" in *Notes on the State of Virginia* (London: John Stockdale, 1787), 229–40, quote on

p. 239. Ibram X. Kendi discusses the history of scientific racism, including Jefferson's ideas and present-day genetics, in *Stamped from the Beginning: The Definitive History of Racism in America* (New York: Bold Type Books: 2016), esp. chaps. 7–12, 36.

28   George Fitzhugh, "The Universal Law of Slavery" (1857), in *Slavery in the United States: A Social, Political, and Historical Encyclopedia*, ed. Junius P. Rodriquez (Santa Barbara, Calif.: ABC-CLIO, 2007), 1: 665–66.

29   See Jenny Bourne, "Slavery in the United States," *EH.Net*, March 28, 2018, https://eh.net/encyclopedia/slavery-in-the-united-states/.

30   Alexander H. Stephens, "Cornerstone Speech" (March 21, 1861), in *The Civil War and Reconstruction: A Documentary Reader*, ed. Stanley Harrold (Malden, Mass.: Blackwell Publishing, 2008), 59–64.

31   "The Book of Negroes" (see fig., p. 55) lists Ralph Henry as "formerly slave to Patrick Henry, Gloucester, Virginia." Several books have erroneously claimed that his enslaver was the famous patriot orator and politician; however, Patrick Henry the Founding Father was from Hanover County and his family had no properties in Gloucester.

32   On the experiences of the Black Loyalists during and after the war, see Cassandra Pybus, *Epic Journeys of Freedom: Runaway Slaves of the American Revolution and Their Global Quest for Liberty* (Boston: Beacon Press, 2006). Pybus discusses Ralph Henry on pages 145, 150, 179–80, and 212.

33   See trial transcriptions in Philip J. Schwarz, *Gabriel's Conspiracy: A Documentary History* (Charlottesville: University of Virginia Press, 2012), 152–53.

34   Manumission deed issued by Jane Minor for Emily Smith and her children, July 31, 1840 (see fig., p. 61).

35   May's deed of manumission for Jane Minor is recorded in the Petersburg Hustings Court Deed Book 7 (1821–1826), 267. For a discussion of Minor and the free Black community of Petersburg, see Suzanne Lebsock, *The Free Women of Petersburg: Status and Culture in a Southern Town, 1784–1860* (New York: W. W. Norton & Company, 1984).

36   For Minor's receipts, see Petersburg Account Books 2 (1825), 141; 3 (1835), 218; 5 (1844), 380; and 4 (1839), 160. Minor—identified as Jincey or Jinsey Snow—appears in Petersburg's *Daily Express* on December 15, 1857, and November 21, 1859. This latter article is the last known record of her.

37   Petersburg Hustings Court Deed Book 11 (1839–1841), 518–19.

38   Lott Cary quoted in John Saillant, ed., "Circular Addressed to the Colored Brethren and Friends in America: An Unpublished Essay by Lott Cary, Sent from Liberia to Virginia, 1827," *Virginia Magazine of History and Biography* 104 (1996): 491.

39   For an overview of the American Colonization Society and Lott Cary, see E. Lee Shepard, Frances S. Pollard, and Janet B. Schwarz, "'The Love of Liberty Brought Us Here': Virginians and the Colonization of Liberia," *Virginia Magazine of History and Biography* 102 (1994): 89–100.

40   Saillant, "Circular Addressed to the Colored Brethren and Friends in America," 492–503.

41   Editorial in the *Colored American*, May 9, 1840, cited in Eric Foner, *Gateway to Freedom: The Hidden History of the Underground Railroad* (New York: W. W. Norton & Company, 2015), 54.

42   Fergus M. Bordewich, *Bound for Canaan: The Underground Railroad and the War for the Soul of America* (New York: Amistad, 2005), 70.

43   *The Confessions of Nat Turner, The Leader of the Late Insurrection in Southampton, Va. As fully and voluntarily made to Thomas R. Gray* (Baltimore: Lucas & Deaver, 1831), 9. Additional sources on Nat Turner's revolt include Patrick Breen, *The Land Shall Be Deluged in Blood: A New History of the Nat Turner Revolt* (New York: Oxford University Press, 2016), and Stephen B. Oates, *The Fires of Jubilee: Nat Turner's Fierce Rebellion* (New York: HarperCollins Publishers, 1975).

44   *The Confessions of Nat Turner*, 9.

45   "The Insurrection, from *The Richmond Whig*," *Virginia Free Press*, September 8, 1831.

46   Cited in Oates, *The Fires of Jubilee*, 105.

47   The most recent and extensive study on the *Creole* revolt and its broader context is Jeffrey R. Kerr-Ritchie, *Rebellious Passage: The* Creole *Revolt and America's Coastal Slave Trade* (Cambridge, UK: Cambridge University Press, 2019). Kerr-Ritchie also corrects earlier counts of 135 enslaved passengers.

48   Kerr-Ritchie, *Rebellious Passage*, 107.

49   "From the Friend of Man: Madison Washington," *The Liberator*, June 10, 1842. Washington was also the subject of Frederick Douglass's novella *The Heroic Slave* (1853). Proslavery publications like the *Richmond Whig* regularly referred to the *Creole* rebels as "murderers and mutineers" (see Kerr-Ritchie, *Rebellious Passage*, 188–90).

50   Maurie D. McInnis, *Slaves Waiting for Sale: Abolitionist Art and the American Slave Trade* (Chicago: University of Chicago Press, 2011), 66.

51   The figures on this graph are drawn from Edward E. Baptist, *The Half Has Never Been Told: Slavery and the Making of American Capitalism* (New York: Basic Books, 2016), 246, and David Brion Davis, "Foreword," in *Econocide: British Slavery in the Era of Abolition*, by Seymour Drescher (Chapel Hill: University of North Carolina Press, 2010), xvii.

52   Henry Box Brown, *Narrative of the Life of Henry Box Brown, Written by Himself* [1851 ed.], introduction by Richard Newman, foreword by Henry Louis Gates, Jr. (New York: Oxford University Press, 2002), 28.

53   Brown, *Narrative*, 60–61.

54   Brown, *Narrative*, 7.

55   Bordewich, *Bound for Canaan*, 324.

56   Cited in Earl Maltz, "Burns, Anthony, The Trial of (1854)," *Encyclopedia Virginia*, last modified February 23, 2021, https://encyclopediavirginia.org/entries/burns-anthony-the-trial-of-1854. See also Maltz's book *Fugitive Slave on Trial: The Anthony Burns Case and Abolitionist Outrage* (Lawrence: University of Kansas Press, 2010) for additional information on Burns's life and trial.

57   Foner, *Gateway to Freedom*, 150.

58   Richard Eppes Diary, 1854–1857, 169–70 (entry for October 13, 1856), Eppes Family Papers, VMHC. In this entry, Eppes refers to her as "Eliza Calwell," but several subsequent records give her name as Sarah; the reason for this discrepancy is unknown.

59   Quote from Richard Eppes Diary, 1852–1854, 77–78 (entry for January 2, 1853). His management approach is discussed and his "Code of Laws" transcribed in Michael L. Nicholls, "'In the Light of Human Beings': Richard Eppes and His Island Plantation Code of Laws," *Virginia Magazine of History and Biography* 89 (1981): 67–78.

60   Cited in F. B. Sanborn, ed., *The Life and Letters of John Brown, Liberator of Kansas, and Martyr of Virginia* (New York: Greenwood Publishing Corp., 1885), 517. For a general overview of John Brown's raid, see William M. S. Rasmussen and Robert S. Tilton, *The Portent: John Brown's Raid in American Memory* (Richmond: Virginia Historical Society, 2009).

61   Harriet Newby to Dangerfield Newby, August 16, 1859. Harriet's letters were found on her husband's body after the raid. They do not survive but were transcribed in the *Governor's Message and Reports of the Public Officers of the State, of the Boards of Directors, and of the Visitors, Superintendents, and Other Agents of Public Instruction or Interests of Virginia* (Richmond, 1859), Library of Virginia, Special Collections.

62   Osborne P. Anderson, *A Voice from Harper's Ferry: A Narrative of Events at Harper's Ferry* (Boston, 1861), 40.

63   From Douglass's speech at Storer College at Harpers Ferry, May 30, 1882, cited in Hannah N. Geffert, "John Brown

and His Black Allies: An Ignored Alliance," *Pennsylvania Magazine of History and Biography* 126 (2002): 610.

64   This entry draws on John David Smith, ed., *Black Soldiers in Blue: African American Troops in the Civil War Era* (Chapel Hill: University of North Carolina Press, 2002), and James S. Price, *The Battle of New Market Heights: Freedom Will Be Theirs by the Sword* (Charleston, S.C.: The History Press, 2011).

65   J. D. Pickens (Texas Brigade), "Fort Harrison," *Confederate Veteran* 21 (1913): 484.

66   Carter Glass, delegate to the constitutional convention, cited in Brent Tarter, *The Grandees of Government: The Origins and Persistence of Undemocratic Politics in Virginia* (Charlottesville: University of Virginia Press, 2013), 267–68.

67   Tarter, *The Grandees of Government*, 268.

68   Jeffrey R. Kerr-Ritchie provides a thorough analysis of Black farmers in post-emancipation Virginia in *Freedpeople in the Tobacco South: Virginia, 1860–1900* (Chapel Hill: University of North Carolina Press, 1999).

69   For a discussion of the Black exodus to urban areas in the late 19th century, see Kerr-Ritchie, *Freedpeople in the Tobacco South*, chap. 8.

70   See Philip Morgan, ed., *"Don't Grieve After Me": The Black Experience in Virginia, 1619– 1986* (Hampton, Va.: Hampton University, 1986), 63.

71   See Phyllis McClure, "Rosenwald Schools," *Encyclopedia Virginia*, last modified December 7, 2020, https://encyclopediavirginia.org/entries/rosenwald-schools.

72   See Brendan Wolfe, "Danville Riot (1883)," *Encyclopedia Virginia*, last modified December 7, 2020, https://encyclopediavirginia.org/entries/danville-riot-1883; and Cameron McWhirter, *Red Summer: The Summer of 1919 and the Awakening of Black America* (New York: Henry Holt & Co., 2011).

73   The Equal Justice Initiative has produced a comprehensive study of lynching: *Lynching in America: Confronting the Legacy of Racial Terror*, 3rd ed. (Montgomery, Ala.: Equal Justice Initiative, 2017), https://eji.org/reports/lynching-in-america/. White supremacists primarily targeted Black people, but they also terrorized Jews, immigrants, labor activists, and others.

74   Antonio T. Bly, "Slave Literacy and Education in Virginia," *Encyclopedia Virginia*, last modified February 1, 2021, https://encyclopediavirginia.org/entries/slave-literacy-and-education-in-virginia.

75   Rev. Lewis C. Lockwood, *Mary S. Peake, The Colored Teacher at Fort Monroe* (Boston:

American Tract Society, 1862), 31. This book and Kay Ann Taylor, "Mary S. Peake and Charlotte L. Forten: Black Teachers during the Civil War and Reconstruction," *Journal of Negro Education* 74 (2005): 124–37, are the best sources on Peake's life.

76   Lockwood, *Mary S. Peake*, 35.

77   Lockwood, *Mary S. Peake*, 64.

78   Good sources on Peter Jacob Carter and Black political participation in the postwar era are Eric Foner, *Freedom's Lawmakers: A Directory of Black Officeholders during Reconstruction* (New York: Oxford University Press, 1993); Luther Porter Jackson, *Negro Office-Holders in Virginia, 1865–1895* (Norfolk, Va.: Guide Quality Press, 1945); and Steven Hahn, *A Nation Under Our Feet: Black Political Struggles in the Rural South from Slavery to the Great Migration* (Cambridge, Mass.: Harvard University Press, 2005).

79   The information in this entry on Virginia's postwar politics is drawn from Jane Elizabeth Dailey, *Before Jim Crow: The Politics of Race in Postemancipation Virginia* (Chapel Hill: University of North Carolina Press, 2000).

80   See W. T. Clark et al., "'Coalition Rule in Danville' (October 1883)," Encyclopedia Virginia, last modified December 7, 2020, https://encyclopediavirginia.org/entries/coalition-rule-in-danville-october-1883.

81   Booker T. Washington, *Up from Slavery: An Autobiography* (New York: A. L. Burt Company, 1901), 53.

82   Booker T. Washington, "Atlanta Exposition Speech," delivered at the Cotton States and International Exposition, Atlanta, Georgia, September 18, 1895, Booker T. Washington Papers, Library of Congress, Washington, D.C.

83   *New York World*, February 22, 1887.

84   *Richmond Planet*, January 30, 1892. The best source on Mitchell's life and career is Ann Field Alexander, *Race Man: The Rise and Fall of the "Fighting Editor," John Mitchell, Jr.* (Charlottesville: University of Virginia Press, 2002). The *Richmond Planet* is available through the Library of Congress, Chronicling America: Historic American Newspapers, https://chroniclingamerica.loc.gov/lccn/sn84025841/.

85   *Richmond Planet*, February 8, 1890.

86   Cited in Alexander, *Race Man*, 42.

87   *Richmond Planet*, April 23, 1904.

88   *Plessy* v. *Ferguson*, 163 U.S. 537 (1896), https://supreme.justia.com/cases/federal/us/163/537/.

89   J. Lee Greene, *Time's Unfading Garden: Anne Spencer's Life and Poetry* (Baton Rouge: Louisiana State University Press, 1977), 164. Greene worked closely with Spencer late in her life to organize her papers; his biography—

which includes her published poems—remains the best source on her life and career.

90   See Greene, *Time's Unfading Garden*, 182.

91   Anne Spencer, "Taboo," Anne Spencer House and Garden Museum, accessed December 11, 2020, http://www.annespencermuseum.com/poetry.php.

92   This essay draws on Brendan Wolfe, "Racial Integrity Laws (1924–1930)," *Encyclopedia Virginia*, last modified February 25, 2021, https://encyclopediavirginia.org/entries/racial-integrity-laws-1924-1930; J. Douglas Smith, *Managing White Supremacy: Race, Politics, and Citizenship in Jim Crow Virginia* (Chapel Hill: University of North Carolina Press, 2002); and Peter Wallenstein, *Tell the Court I Love My Wife: Race, Marriage, and Law—An American History* (New York: Palgrave Macmillan, 2002).

93   See Gregory Michael Dorr, *Segregation's Science: Eugenics and Society in Virginia* (Charlottesville: University of Virginia Press, 2004).

94   Cited in Wallenstein, *Tell the Court I Love My Wife*, 223.

95   *Loving* v. *Virginia*, 388 U.S. 1 (1967), https://www.law.cornell.edu/supremecourt/text/388/1.

96   Isabel Wilkerson, *The Warmth of Other Suns: The Epic Story of America's Great Migration* (New York: Random House, 2010), 534; Peter Wallenstein, *Cradle of America: Four Centuries of Virginia History* (Lawrence: University Press of Kansas, 2007), 258.

97   Mary Johnson Sprow Diary, cited in Elizabeth Clark-Lewis, "'Fast Living': The Diary of Mary Johnson Sprow, Domestic Worker," *Washington History* 5 (Spring/Summer 1993): 49.

98   Clark-Lewis, "'Fast Living,'" 47.

99   Mary Johnson Sprow Diary, October 1 and November 7, 1916, cited in Clark-Lewis, "'Fast Living,'" 56, 57.

100   Author's conversation with Elizabeth Clark-Lewis.

101   General H. H. Arnold, Commanding General, Army Air Forces, to Ruth Givings (Clemenceau's mother), May 16, 1944, Clemenceau Givings Scrapbook, VMHC.

102   Major General H. E. Ely, Memorandum for the Chief of Staff, Subject: Employment of Negro Man Power in War, 2 incls., November 10, 1925, FDR Presidential Library and Museum, https://www.fdrlibrary.org/documents/356632/390886/tusk_doc_a.pdf/4693156a-8844-4361-ae17-03407e7a3dee.

103   2nd Lt. Clemenceau Givings to Noel and Ruth Givings (his parents), January 18, 1944, Clemenceau Givings Scrapbook, VMHC.

104   "Clem Givings Was Just a Jolly Good

Fellow," unidentified newspaper clipping, 1944, Clemenceau Givings Scrapbook, VMHC. This Scrapbook provides the best source on the life and service of Clemenceau Givings; for information on the Tuskegee Airmen, see J. Todd Moye, *Freedom Flyers: The Tuskegee Airmen of World War II* (New York: Oxford University Press, 2010).

105   Parts of this entry appeared earlier in Karen Sherry, "Artifact Spotlight: Tuskegee Airman Scrapbook," *Richmond Times-Dispatch*, February 15, 2020.

106   Arnold Rampersad, ed., *The Collected Poems of Langston Hughes* (New York: Knopf, 1994), 281.

107   For information on these and other civil rights activities in Virginia, see Simon Hall, "Civil Rights Activism in 1960s Virginia," *Journal of Black Studies* 38, no. 2 (2007): 251–67.

108   Emmett Till, Medgar Evers, and Dr. Martin Luther King, Jr., were among the forty-one people murdered by white supremacists between 1954 and 1968, while another seventy-five civil rights activists died under suspicious circumstances. These individuals are commemorated—and additional information is available—at the Southern Poverty Law Center's Civil Rights Memorial in Montgomery, Alabama, https://www.splcenter.org/civil-rights-memorial.

109   Ironically, Howard Smith, a U.S. Congressman from Virginia and staunch civil rights opponent, added "sex" as a protected category for employment, expecting that this amendment would doom the bill but ultimately giving the Civil Rights Act of 1964 a more expansive definition of equality—and providing impetus to the burgeoning feminist movement.

110   Bayard Rustin described the evolution of the civil rights movement with this phrase in "From Protest to Politics: The Future of the Civil Rights Movement," *Commentary* 39, no. 2 (February 1965), available online through ULS Digital Collections, University of Pittsburgh, https://digital.library.pitt.edu/islandora/object/pitt%3A31735066227830.

111   United States Census Bureau, "Black Persons by Poverty Status in 1969, 1979, 1989, and 1999," https://www.census.gov/data/tables/time-series/dec/cph-series/cph-l/cph-l-166.html.

112   On the Black Panther Party, see Joshua Bloom and Waldo E. Martin, Jr., *Black Against Empire: The History and Politics of the Black Panther Party* (Berkeley: University of California Press, 2016).

113   For information on these and all Black Congressional representatives, see "People Search," History, Art & Archives, United States House of Representatives, https://history.house.gov/People/Search. Throughout

its history, only eleven Black people—none from Virginia—have served in the U.S. Senate to date, see "African American Senators," Art & History, United States Senate, https://www.senate.gov/pagelayout/history/h_multi_sections_and_teasers/Photo_Exhibit_African_American_Senators.htm.

114   Republican political strategist Lee Atwater infamously described this coded language of the Southern strategy in a 1981 interview as follows: "You start out in 1954 by saying 'N*****, n*****, n*****.' By 1968 you can't say 'n*****'—that hurts you. Backfires. So you say stuff like forced busing, states' rights and all that stuff." Quoted in Craig S. Pascoe, Karen Trahan Leathem, and Andy Ambrose, eds., *The American South in the Twentieth Century* (Athens: University of Georgia Press, 2005), 230.

115   In his 1976 and 1980 presidential campaigns, Ronald Reagan used this phrase to describe a woman who fraudulently collected welfare benefits as part of his call for welfare reform. The term became a racialized dog whistle based on popular racist stereotypes linking poverty and Blackness and portraying welfare recipients as lazy, sexually promiscuous, unwed mothers undeserving of public assistance. See Ann Cammett, "Deadbeat Dads and Welfare Queens: How Metaphor Shapes Poverty Law," *Boston College Journal of Law and Social Justice* 34, no. 2 (May 2014): 243–44, https://lawdigitalcommons.bc.edu/jlsj/vol34/iss2/3.

116   On race and the criminal justice system, see Michelle Alexander, *The New Jim Crow: Mass Incarceration in the Age of Colorblindness* (New York: The New Press, 2020)—statistics cited here are on pp. 76 and 123—and The Sentencing Project, *Report to the United Nations on Racial Disparities in the U.S. Criminal Justice System* (Washington, D.C.: The Sentencing Project, 2018), https://www.sentencingproject.org/publications/un-report-on-racial-disparities. Alexander describes this form of institutionalized racism as a new form of Jim Crow for controlling and oppressing Black Americans.

117   As Ta-Nehisi Coates succinctly wrote, "if [Obama's] very existence inflamed America's racist conscience, it also expanded the country's anti-racist imagination." In "My President Was Black: A History of the First African American White House—and of What Came Next," *Atlantic*, January/February 2017, 53, https://www.theatlantic.com/magazine/archive/2017/01/my-president-was-black/508793. For additional analysis of the Obama presidency and race, see Michael Eric Dyson, *The Black Presidency: Barack Obama and the Politics of Race in America* (Boston: Houghton Mifflin Harcourt, 2016).

118   The Southern Poverty Law Center (SPLC), which has been monitoring hate

crimes since the 1980s, declared 2011 as an all-time high for the number of hate groups. See Mark Potok, "The Year in Hate and Extremism," *Intelligence Report* (SPLC), February 15, 2017, https://www.splcenter.org/fighting-hate/intelligence-report/2017/year-hate-and-extremism. See also Wesley Lowery, Kimberly Kindy, and Andrew Ba Tran, "In the United States, Right-Wing Violence Is on the Rise," *Washington Post*, November 25, 2018.

119   Two online sources that compile recent research on racial disparities are Hedwig Lee et al., "The Demographics of Racial Inequality in the United States," Brookings Institution, July 27, 2020, https://www.brookings.edu/blog/up-front/2020/07/27/the-demographics-of-racial-inequality-in-the-united-states; and Shayanne Gal et al., "26 Simple Charts to Show Friends and Family Who Aren't Convinced Racism Is Still a Problem in America," *Business Insider*, July 8, 2020, https://www.businessinsider.com/us-systemic-racism-in-charts-graphs-data-2020-6.

120   For a discussion of the history and significance of Confederate symbols, as well as statistics on their number and location, see the Southern Poverty Law Center report *Whose Heritage? Public Symbols of the Confederacy* (Montgomery, Ala.: Southern Poverty Law Center, 2019), https://www.splcenter.org/20190201/whose-heritage-public-symbols-confederacy#executive-summary. Another online resource is "On Monument Avenue," created by the American Civil War Museum, Richmond, https://onmonumentave.com.

121   Although Trump condemned bigotry in other remarks, this statement—viewed as creating a false equivalency between the white supremacists and antiracist protesters and further emboldening white supremacist groups—drew criticism from across the political spectrum. See Hawes Spencer, *Summer of Hate: Charlottesville, USA* (Charlottesville: University of Virginia Press, 2019), 132–37.

122   For data on the police killing of Black Americans and the names of the more than 1,900 victims since 2015, see Mapping Police Violence, https://mappingpoliceviolence.org, and "The Police Shootings Database, 2015–2021," *Washington Post*, https://www.washingtonpost.com/graphics/investigations/police-shootings-database.

123   On the movement and its critics, see the BLM website, https://blacklivesmatter.com, and Juliet Hooker, "Black Lives Matter and the Paradoxes of U.S. Black Politics: From Democratic Sacrifice to Democratic Repair," *Political Theory* 44, no. 4 (2016): 448–69, https://doi.org/10.1177/0090591716640314.

124   Barbara Johns, "Recollections" (undated), in *A Little Child Shall Lead Them: A Documentary Account of the Struggle*

for School Desegregation in Prince Edward County, Virginia, ed. Brian J. Daugherity and Brian Grogan (Charlottesville: University of Virginia Press, 2019), 45.

125   A few good sources on Barbara Johns and the school desegregation fight are R. C. Smith, *They Closed Their Schools: Prince Edward County, Virginia, 1951–1964* (Chapel Hill: University of North Carolina Press, 1965), Brian J. Daugherity, *Keep On Keeping On: The NAACP and the Implementation of Brown v. Board of Education in Virginia* (Charlottesville: University of Virginia Press, 2016), and George Lewis, *Massive Resistance: The White Response to the Civil Rights Movement*, rev. 2nd ed. (Lanham, Md.: Rowman & Littlefield Publishers, 2006).

126   *Brown* v. *Board of Education of Topeka, Kansas*, 347 U.S. 483 (1954), https://supreme.justia.com/cases/federal/us/347/483/.

127   Virginia State Senator Garland Gray made this claim, cited in William G. Thomas, "Virginia's 'Massive Resistance' to School Desegregation," The Civil Rights Movement, *Digital Resources for United States History*, (Charlottesville: Virginia Center for Digital History and the Miller Center of Public Affairs, University of Virginia, 2005), http://www.vcdh.virginia.edu/solguide/VUS13/essay13a.html.

128   *Charles Green* v. *County School Board of New Kent County, Virginia*, 391 U.S. 430 (1968), https://supreme.justia.com/cases/federal/us/391/430/.

129   Rev. Wyatt Tee Walker, "Petitioning Statement for Integrated Library Facilities before City Council of Petersburg, VA," June 17, 1959, 3, Dr. and Mrs. Wyatt Tee Walker Collection, University of Richmond.

130   Oral History of the Rev. Dr. Wyatt Tee Walker and Mrs. Theresa Ann Walker, interview by Joseph Evans, transcript, July 29, 2016, 23, Dr. and Mrs. Wyatt Tee Walker Oral Histories, University of Richmond.

131   Oral History, 47.

132   Walker, quoted in Raymond Pierre Hylton, "Intersection of Change," *Style Weekly* (Richmond), November 5, 2008.

133   Elizabeth U. Cascio and Ebonya Washington, "Valuing the Vote: The Redistribution of Voting Rights and State Funds Following the Voting Rights Act of 1965," *Quarterly Journal of Economics* 129 (2014): 380.

134   Quoted in Cathy Dyson, "Gladys West's Work on GPS 'Would Impact the World,'" *Free Lance-Star* (Fredericksburg), January 19, 2018.

135   The phrase "hidden figures" comes from the title of Margot Lee Shetterly's book, *Hidden Figures: The American Dream and the Untold Story of the Black Women Mathematicians Who Helped Win the Space Race* (New York: William Morrow, 2016), and the related film, which first brought to light the untold story of the female mathematicians working at NASA in Langley, Virginia, in the mid-20th century.

136   Dr. Gladys B. West and M. H. Jackson, *It Began with a Dream* (Dahlgren, Va.: IGWEST Publishing, 2020), 117. This autobiography provides the most comprehensive source of West's life and career.

137   West and Jackson, *It Began with a Dream*, 92; West quoted in Dyson, "Gladys West's Work on GPS."

138   Quoted in Raymond Arsenault, *Arthur Ashe: A Life* (New York: Simon & Schuster, 2018), 136. This biography is a good resource on Ashe's life and career.

139   Arthur Ashe, *Days of Grace: A Memoir* (New York: Alfred A. Knopf, 1993), 126.

140   Cascio and Washington, "Valuing the Vote," 380.

141   L. Douglas Wilder, *Son of Virginia: A Life in America's Political Arena* (Guilford, Conn.: Lyons Press, 2015), 39.

142   Quotations from Wilder, *Son of Virginia*, 51, 53.

143   During Reconstruction, P. B. S. Pinchback served as Louisiana's acting governor for less than one month in 1872, when the standing governor was facing impeachment charges. Wilder was the first Black man to win a popular election for governor, followed by Deval Patrick of Massachusetts in 2006.

144   The information on Missy Elliott's career and feminist impact in this essay is drawn from Nikki Lane, "Black Women Queering the Mic: Missy Elliott Disturbing the Boundaries of Racialized Sexuality and Gender," *Journal of Homosexuality* 58 (2011): 775–92; Candace McDuffie, "20 Years of 'Supa Dupa Fly': How Missy Elliott Singlehandedly Changed the Rap Game for Women," *Vibe*, July 15, 2017, https://www.vibe.com/2017/07/missy-elliott-supa-dupa-fly-anniversary; and Kat George, "Why Missy Elliott's Feminist Legacy Is Criminally Underrated," *Dazed*, January 22, 2016, https://www.dazeddigital.com/music/article/29353/1/why-missy-elliott-s-feminist-legacy-is-criminally-underrated.

145   Queen Zakia Shabazz, "Virginia Must Work toward Environmental Justice," *Virginian-Pilot*, June 18, 2020.

146   Robert D. Bullard et al., *Toxic Wastes and Race at Twenty, 1987–2007* (Cleveland, Ohio: United Church of Christ, 2007), x, 4, available on the NRDC (Natural Resources Defense Council) website at https://www.nrdc.org/sites/default/files/toxic-wastes-and-race-at-twenty-1987-2007.pdf. For more on environmental racism, see Brendan Coolsaet, ed., *Environmental Justice: Key Issues* (New York: Routledge, 2020).

147   Information about Shabazz and her activism is from the author's conversations with Shabazz, and from "Queen Zakia Shabazz," biography, United Parents Against Lead (UPAL) website, 2019, https://www.upal.org/zakia-shabazz-bio.

148   Zyhna Bryant, "Beyond the Hashtag: How to Take Anti-Racist Action in Your Life," *Teen Vogue*, June 8, 2020, https://www.teenvogue.com/story/beyond-the-hashtag-how-to-take-anti-racist-action. For additional sources on Zyahna Bryant, see her website at https://zybryant.com.

149   "Change the Name of Lee Park and Remove the Statue," petition to Charlottesville City Council, Change.org, 2016, https://www.change.org/p/charlottesville-city-council-change-the-name-of-lee-park-and-remove-the-statue-in-charlottesville-va.

150   Bryant, "Beyond the Hashtag."

151   Information in this essay is drawn from the author's conversations with Bellen Woodard and her family, and from Nicole Tocco, "A Color for Everyone," *Scholastic News*, August 31, 2020, https://sn3.scholastic.com/issues/2020-21/083120/a-color-for-everyone.html#On%20Level.

152   Dr. Joy Lawson Davis (@davis_joy), " @BellenTheBee, I told my 7yrold grandson Dylan your story, when he looked at your multicultural crayons, he said 'that's my Dad' as he pointed to the SERENGETI crayon!! I teared up…just imagining how important these crayons will be to kids worldwide!!" Twitter, October 8, 2020, 9:38 p.m., https://twitter.com/davis_joy/status/1314304128647155713.

153   President Barack Obama, "Remarks by the President in Eulogy for the Honorable Reverend Clementa Pickney," June 26, 2015, https://obamawhitehouse.archives.gov/the-press-office/2015/06/26/remarks-president-eulogy-honorable-reverend-clementa-pinckney.

BIBLIOGRAPHY

Following is a brief list of some of the key online and published resources for those readers interested in learning more about the topics covered in *Determined*. This is by no means an exhaustive bibliography, as the body of scholarship on Black history is extensive and ever-expanding, but the resources cited here and in the endnotes throughout this book provide a good starting point for additional study.

Online Resources

1619 Project, *New York Times Magazine*, https://www.nytimes.com/interactive/2019/08/14/magazine/1619-america-slavery.html

African American Resources, Virginia Memory, Library of Virginia, https://www.virginiamemory.com/collections/collections_by_topic

Black History, Virginia Museum of History & Culture, https://www.VirginiaHistory.org/BlackHistory

Encyclopedia Virginia, Virginia Humanities, https://www.encyclopediavirginia.org

Talking About Race, National Museum of African American History and Culture, Smithsonian Institution, https://nmaahc.si.edu/learn/talking-about-race

Published Resources

Alexander, Michelle. *The New Jim Crow: Mass Incarceration in the Age of Colorblindness*. 10th anniv. ed. New York: The New Press, 2020.

Ayers, Edward L. *The Thin Light of Freedom: The Civil War and Emancipation in the Hearth of America*. New York: W. W. Norton & Company, 2003.

Blassingame, John W. *Slave Testimony: Two Centuries of Letters, Speeches, Interviews, and Autobiographies*. Baton Rouge: Louisiana State University Press, 1977.

Blight, David. *Race and Reunion: The Civil War in American Memory*. Cambridge, Mass.: Belknap Press, 2001.

Brasher, Glenn David. *The Peninsula Campaign and the Necessity of Emancipation: African Americans and the Fight for Freedom*. Chapel Hill: University of North Carolina Press, 2012.

Breen, T. H., and Stephen Innes. *"Myne Owne Ground": Race and Freedom on Virginia's Eastern Shore, 1640–1676*. New York: Oxford University Press, 1980.

Brown, Leslie, ed. *African American Voices: A Documentary Reader from Emancipation to the Present*. Hoboken, N.J.: Wiley Blackwell Publishing, 2014.

Campbell, Benjamin. *Richmond's Unhealed History*. Richmond: Brandylane Publishers, 2012.

Campbell, Edward D. C., Jr., and Kym S. Rice, eds. *Before Freedom Came: African-American Life in the Antebellum South*. Charlottesville: University Press of Virginia, 1991.

Dailey, Jane Elizabeth. *Before Jim Crow: The Politics of Race in Postemancipation Virginia*. Chapel Hill: University of North Carolina Press, 2000.

Deyle, Stephen. *Carry Me Back: The Domestic Slave Trade in American Life*. New York: Oxford University Press, 2005.

Dudziak, Mary. *Cold War Civil Rights: Race and the Image of American Democracy*. Princeton: Princeton University Press, 2000.

Egerton, Douglas R. *Death or Liberty: African Americans and Revolutionary America*. New York: Oxford University Press, 2009.

Gaines, Kevin. *Uplifting the Race: Black Leadership, Politics, and Culture in the Twentieth Century*. Chapel Hill: University of North Carolina Press, 1996.

Gates, Henry Louis, Jr. *Stony the Road: Reconstruction, White Supremacy, and the Rise of Jim Crow*. New York: Penguin Press, 2019.

Ham, Deborah Newman, ed. *The African American Odyssey*. Washington, D.C.: Library of Congress, 1998.

Hayter, Julian Maxwell. *The Dream Is Lost: Voting Rights and the Politics of Race in Richmond, Virginia.* Lexington: University Press of Kentucky, 2017.

Horton, James Oliver, and Lois E. Horton. *Hard Road to Freedom: The Story of African America.* New Brunswick, N.J.: Rutgers University Press, 2001.

Jordan, Winthrop D. *White over Black: American Attitudes toward the Negro, 1550–1812.* Chapel Hill: University of North Carolina Press, 1968.

Joseph, Penial E. *Waiting 'Til the Midnight Hour: A Narrative History of Black Power in America.* New York: Henry Holt & Company, 2007.

Kendi, Ibram X. *Stamped from the Beginning: The Definitive History of Racism in America.* New York: Bold Type Books: 2016.

Kerr-Ritchie, Jeffrey R. *Freedpeople in the Tobacco South: Virginia, 1860–1900.* Chapel Hill: University of North Carolina Press, 1999.

Kilson, Martin. *Transformation of the African American Intelligentsia, 1880–2012.* Cambridge, Mass.: Harvard University Press, 2014.

Kirk, John A., ed. *The Civil Rights Movement: A Documentary Reader.* Hoboken, N.J.: Wiley Blackwell Publishing, 2020.

Kulikoff, Allan. *Tobacco and Slaves: The Development of Southern Cultures in the Chesapeake, 1680–1800.* Chapel Hill: University of North Carolina Press, 1986.

Link, William A. *Roots of Secession: Slavery and Politics in Antebellum Virginia.* Chapel Hill: University of Virginia Press, 2003.

Marble, Manning. *Race, Reform, and Rebellion: The Second Reconstruction and Beyond in Black America, 1945–2006.* 3rd ed. Jackson: University Press of Mississippi, 2007.

Morgan, Edmund S. *American Slavery, American Freedom: The Ordeal of Colonial Virginia.* New York: W. W. Norton & Company, 1975.

Morgan, Philip, ed. *"Don't Grieve after Me": The Black Experience in Virginia, 1619–1986.* Hampton, Va.: Hampton University, 1986.

Muhammad, Khalil. *The Condemnation of Blackness: Race, Crime, and the Making of Modern Urban America.* Cambridge, Mass.: Harvard University Press, 2019.

Musselwhite, Paul, Peter C. Mancall, and James Horn, eds. *Virginia 1619: Slavery and Freedom in the Making of English America.* Chapel Hill: University of North Carolina Press, 2019.

Nelson, Louis P., and Claudrena N. Harold, eds. *Charlottesville 2017: The Legacy of Race and Inequity.* Charlottesville: University of Virginia Press, 2018.

Parent, Anthony S., Jr. *Foul Means: The Formation of a Slave Society in Virginia, 1660–1740.* Chapel Hill: University of North Carolina Press, 2003.

Smith, J. Douglas, *Managing White Supremacy: Race, Politics, and Citizenship in Jim Crow Virginia.* Chapel Hill: University of North Carolina Press, 2002.

Spencer, Hawes. *Summer of Hate: Charlottesville, USA.* Charlottesville: University of Virginia Press, 2018.

Tarter, Brent. *Gerrymanders: How Redistricting Has Protected Slavery, White Supremacy, and Partisan Minorities in Virginia.* Charlottesville: University of Virginia Press, 2019.

———. *Virginians and Their Histories.* Charlottesville: University of Virginia Press, 2020.

Taylor, Alan. *The Internal Enemy: Slavery and War in Virginia, 1772–1832.* New York: W. W. Norton & Company, 2013.

Taylor, Keeanga-Yamahtta. *From #BlackLivesMatter to Black Liberation.* Chicago: Haymarket Books, 2016.

Tyler-McGraw, Marie, and Gregg D. Kimball. *In Bondage and Freedom: Antebellum Black Life in Richmond, Virginia.* Richmond: Valentine Museum, 1988.

Wallenstein, Peter. *Blue Laws and Black Codes: Conflict, Courts, and Change in Twentieth-Century Virginia.* Charlottesville: University of Virginia Press, 2004.

Whittaker, Matthew C. *Peace Be Still: Modern Black America from World War II to Barack Obama.* Lincoln: University of Nebraska Press, 2013.

Wilkerson, Isabel. *The Warmth of Other Suns: The Epic Story of America's Great Migration.* New York: Random House, 2010.

INDEX

PICTURE CREDITS

Front cover (top): Students protesting school closings in Farmville, Prince Edward County, July 1963. Richmond Times-Dispatch

Front cover (bottom): Antiracism demonstration in Charlottesville, August 12, 2018. Erin Schaff / The New York Times / Redux

Back cover: Company E, 4th U.S. Colored Infantry, at Fort Lincoln, Washington, D.C., 1863–1865. Library of Congress

Front flap: "Nat Turner and His Confederates in Council," illustration from Orville J. Victor, *History of American Conspiracies* (New York: James D. Torrey, 1863). Schomburg Center for Research in Black Culture, The New York Public Library, 1229308

Back flap: Black students with teacher James Heywood Blackwell, late 19th century. The Valentine

Frontispiece: Presidential candidate Barack Obama at a campaign rally in Virginia Beach, October 30, 2008. Getty Images

p. 4: *Slaves in Court 1741*, 19th century, illustration. Granger

p. 14: Organizer Quiara Holmes (center) and other protesters in march for racial justice in Richmond, May 31, 2020. Photo: Crixell Matthews / VPM News

pp. 18–19: Illustration of a tobacco plantation from "The History and Mystery of Tobacco," *Harper's New Monthly Magazine*, 1855.

pp. 46–47: "Nat Turner and His Confederates in Council," illustration from Orville J. Victor, *History of American Conspiracies* (New York: James D. Torrey, 1863). Schomburg Center for Research in Black Culture, The New York Public Library, 1229308

pp. 92–93: A segregated bus, photographed by Stan Wayman, from *Life*, May 7, 1956.

pp. 126–27: Civil rights protesters outside the White House, March 12, 1965. Library of Congress